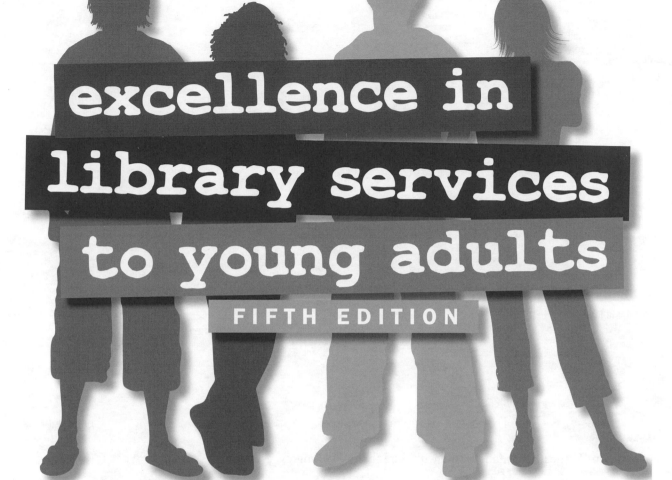

excellence in library services to young adults

FIFTH EDITION

Edited by Amy Alessio for the

Young Adult Library Services Association

Young Adult Library Services Association

A division of the

American Library Association

Chicago

June 2008

Cataloging-in-Publication data is on file with the Library of Congress.

Design and composition by AgdR publishing services

The paper used in this publication meets the minimum requirements of American National Standard for Information Sciences—Permanence of Paper for Printed Library Materials, ANSI-Z39.48-1992 ♾

ISBN13: 978-0-8389-8457-4

Printed in the United States of America

CONTENTS

Seven

PREFACE
by Mary K. Chelton

I am delighted to see a superb YALSA-produced publication that documents and disseminates YA services ideas continue into its fifth edition, ably edited by Amy Alessio, especially one started by Hardy Franklin, an ALA president now deceased, who loaned his name, his presidential theme, and his presidential program to services to young adults. Of all his many activities, the Excellence series may justifiably be considered both his legacy and that of Margaret Edwards, the Enoch Pratt Free Library's famous YA coordinator, whose Trust has funded the project to date.

As the person who edited the first three Excellence books, (albeit with the help of some great library school students), I'm very glad to see the program categories updated here. The addition of white papers on relevant topics such as teen spaces and the value of young adult literature, as well as the inclusion of specific resources listed under programs, extend the value of the content for continuing education for YA practitioners. The program categories, such as "YA Spaces "and "Services under $100," underscore both the growth and residual reality of YA services at the same time. As a personal fan of *American Idol* who is fascinated with the incredibly talented teens like Jordin Sparks (winner of the 2007 contest), and 17-year-old David Archuleta competing in 2008, I particularly appreciated San José Public Library's Teen Idol singing contest, as a great way to involve YAs in the library, capitalize on their popular culture interests, and show off their considerable talent at the same time.

YA interest in technology is apparent in both the content and publicity of the programs described. Whether it is the Cheshire Public Library's Teen Podcast, the Louisville Free Public Library's AnimeCon, the use of audiobooks at the Virginia School for the Deaf and Blind, or just the fact that every program or program entry form was posted on a library Web site or advertised on MySpace make the point repeatedly.

One of the most politically wise inclusions in this edition is the new subcategory within each program description called "Relevance to Overall Young Adult Services," where the program authors have to state how this program advances the total program, not only YA in some cases, but also the entire library. The need to clarify this relationship grounds any particular program within its particular library's mission, and keeps the librarian's eye on the goals of the service.

Another important, but almost inadvertent inclusion is the number of times program descriptors acknowledge that what they are doing is positive youth development. This is a major goal of YA services as outlined in *New Directions in Library Services to Young Adults*, another excellent (pun intended) YALSA publication by Patrick Jones, which is based on work on youth developmental assets by the Search Institute in Minneapolis.

The sheer diversity of the youth population often necessitates an emphasis on mutual understanding across cultural boundaries, and the new category of programs called "Living in a Diverse World" recognizes this reality, not only with programs like in Hennepin County, but also because or the many times other programs are cross-listed under this heading.

The overwhelming popularity of creating physical and virtual spaces in conjunction with teen input that YAs can call their own in local libraries, creates a "text" written in both real and cyberspace architecture that says that young adults are not only welcome, but also have unique needs that are recognized. Many good examples are included, from the Teen Artist of the Month in Alachua County Library in Gainesville, Florida, to the Teen Podcast Program in the Cheshire Public Library in Cheshire, Connecticut, to the Teen Corner makeover in the Randolph County Public Library in Asheboro, North Carolina. I suspect that this is not the last time this category will be used.

This monograph also continues the emphasis on evaluation and documentation pioneered in earlier volumes, thus adding this to help those wishing to emulate or replicate the programs get a head start, besides giving contact person information and suggested program variations.

The Excellence series continues in good form with augmented and updated content that once again captures the inventiveness and joy of young adult services.

ACKNOWLEDGMENTS

The Excellence in Library Services for Young Adults project is a team effort, and this fifth round, including the fifth edition of this namesake book, is no exception. Many people made the publication and promotion of *Excellence in Library Services to Young Adults*, fifth edition, possible.

The publication of this book and the award prizes to those who created these wonderful programs and services would not be possible without the Margaret A. Edwards Trust. The trustees for this fund continue Margaret's vision of excellence and enthusiasm for service to young adults with their generous support of the Young Adult Library Services Association (YALSA) and the initiatives it offers, such as Excellence.

Thanks go also to Dr. Mary K. Chelton, an accomplished advocate for young adults through her writing and teaching, for her inspired preface to this edition. Her work on the first three editions of *Excellence in Library Services to Young Adults* continues to influence those of us who edited future volumes.

Renee Vaillancourt McGrath, editor of the fourth edition, offered much appreciated advice and encouragement when the work began on this one.

The work of YALSA is coordinated by a crack team of dedicated staff, including Executive Director Beth Yoke, Program Officer Nichole Gilbert, Communications Specialist Stephanie Kuenn, and Administrative Assistant Letitia Smith. This edition would not be possible without their care and patience, from promoting the program, collecting the submissions, working with the judges, shaping the publication, and championing the project.

Selecting the winning programs and services was a challenge led by dedicated YALSA members who formed a jury. Chair RoseMary Honnold, Coshocton (Ohio) Public Library; Roxy Ekstrom, Schaumburg Township (Ill.) Library; Carol Marlowe, Rahway (N.J.) Public Library; Jessica Mize, Ohio; and Mary Anne Nichols, Kent State University, Ohio.

Of course the very high caliber of programs and services would not be possible without the YALSA members who created them. Acknowledgments are certainly due to every person who entered a program or service for consideration and especially to the twenty-five programs selected to exemplify excellence in library services for young adults. In addition to their hard work serving teens, the winners helped make this book useful by submitting further details, pictures, and handouts—making it easier for readers to recreate those initiatives in their own communities for young adults.—Amy Alessio, editor

INTRODUCTION

by Amy Alessio

*E*diting the descriptions of twenty-five such excellent programs was an inspiring and pleasurable task. My work at the Schaumburg Township District Library in Illinois for more than a decade has taught me that teens need and want to use their libraries, either in school or in a public library setting. How can the library staff get them there? How can the library staff help teens meet their needs on their journey to becoming healthy adults? That task is harder, and the winning initiatives described below achieved this at exciting levels in their respective communities.

Sponsored by the Young Adult Library Services Association (YALSA) and the Margaret A. Edwards Trust, the Excellence program reminds us that encouraging teens to read for pleasure, to find joy and purpose with library initiatives, and to help the library in these tasks, is something libraries can always invite teens to do.

The Excellence in Library Services to Young Adults Task Force of the YALSA honored twenty-five exemplary teen programs or services in all types of libraries. The top five programs received cash awards of $1,000 each. Twenty "best of the rest" applications received cash awards of $250.

Applications were turned into the YALSA office by June 1, 2007. Winners were selected by a task force comprised of Chair Rosemary Honnold, and members Roxy Ekstrom, Carol Marlowe, Jessica Mize, and Mary Anne Nichols. Winners were selected based upon the following criteria:

> The degree to which the program or service meets the needs of its community, particularly the young adult audience specified. (10 points)
>
> The originality of the program or service (creative, innovative, unique). (20 points)
>
> The degree to which the program or service reflects the concepts identified in *New Directions for Library Service to Young Adults* (Jones 2002). (20 points)
>
> The degree to which the program or service impacts and improves service to young adults. (25 points)

The quality of the program or service (well planned, well marketed, well organized, well implemented, and well evaluated). (25 points)

Definitions

For the purposes of the application, the following definitions applied:

Services—a term for all of the activities offered by libraries for users.

Program—a library-sponsored event, inside or outside the library, which appeals to a group rather than an individual. A program can be informational, recreational, educational, or all three.

Young adults—young people between the ages of 12 and 18; students in middle school, junior high, or high school.

Public library—an agency established by a municipality, county, or region to provide library resources and services to all residents in that jurisdiction.

School library media center—an agency that provides services and programs in either public or private schools. The programs and services can be offered in a single school or throughout the district. They must be specifically planned for students in middle, junior, or senior high schools.

Institutional library—a library maintained by a public or private institution to serve its staff and persons in its care.

Community agency—either government or private agency that promotes the welfare of the audience.

Applicants were asked to summarize the program or service and describe their library, as well as lay out specifics about the program and its costs. They also discussed the specific audience, as well as the demographics of the area their libraries serve, as well as marketing their program or service, how many young adults they reached, how much staff time was involved, and other details. (See appendix A, "Application for Fifth Round of Excellence in Library Services to Young Adults.")

Categories

Categories are chosen with a view to honoring classic teen programs and inspiring people with new, innovative ideas. It is hard to predetermine what will be popular, and in this set of twenty-five winners, no categories were submitted for the Teen Tech Week™ programs, and only one for the promotion of award-winning young adult literature. That said, there are several other programs that could be used or adapted to fit those categories. It could be that Teen Tech Week was too new of a category to garner award-winning initiatives, as the first one was held in 2007. As with any program book, these are meant to inspire and to be adapted to any school or public library. No one situation will fit all library situations or all budgets! Successful teen services professionals are used to this kind of creativity—often starting teen services from scratch or with a new group of teens every few years. There will be plenty to inspire in this volume.

Categories were listed on the application materials as follows:

1. Enhancing teen spaces, physical or virtual—this includes teen space makeovers, Web-based services or programs for teens and/or projects that make libraries in schools and public sectors more teen friendly and/or accessible.

2. Teen Tech Week—educational or recreational programs or services relating to YALSA's inaugural Teen Tech Week held March 4–10, 2007.

3. Creative teen clubs—regularly-meeting teen groups based on a teen interest or those that enhance library or literary experiences for teens.

4. Promotion of award-winning young adult literature—services or programs that fea-

ture any of YALSA's awards: Alex Awards, Margaret Edwards Award, and/or the Michael Printz Award.

5. Reading raves—unique reading promotion initiatives, in the areas of readers' advisory, book discussion groups, incorporation of youth participation in library reading programs, services to reluctant readers or special needs readers, and so on.

6. Community connections—programs or services that involve a close partnership with schools, public libraries, or agencies in the community.

7. Living in a diverse world—services or programs to teens that promote respect for differences and/or reach out to teens of diverse backgrounds, such as ethnicity, language, sexual orientation, learning and communication styles, gender, disability, or economic status.

8. Services under $100—high impact services or programs that are low in cost.

9. Special events—a program or service that runs no more than twice a year and has high interest or high impact on area teens.

Format

Application materials were used to compile this book, in addition to extra supplemental material requested from each winning program coordinator in fall 2007. Each winner was asked to provide further information about each program, such as steps involved in execution, suggested changes, variations, and photos and reproducible handouts where possible to make offering or adapting these programs as easy as possible. The responses vary in detail provided, as some programs can be broken down into specific steps with variations better than others. Under each category, programs are listed in alphabetical order based on the name of the school or public library. Under each program, readers will find the following information, which matches the application:

Title of the program/service

Name of library system, school district, or institutional library

Type of program/service: Was it a series or a one time event?

Targeted audiences: Who was this program intended for? Different ages of teens, or special audiences such as at-risk teens?

Name of contact person

Other categories for this program: Where else in the Excellence application categories might this program fit?

Program summary

Steps: Some programs offer a breakdown of steps that occurred in the planning and execution of this program.

Description of library or school

Intended audience and demographics

Rationale: Why is this program important for excellent library services to young adults?

Numbers of young adults reached

Numbers of staff and volunteers

Funding and budget figures

Marketing

Youth participation

Evaluation: Some programs offer suggested changes to the way the program occurred.

Suggested variations: The information provided for some programs offer other ways to offer similar events on different scales or in different settings.

Relevance to overall young adult services at institution: Excellent programs are usually the result of a strong overall dedication to young adult services. How did this program fit into other library services?

Resources: Some programs were based upon ideas from other resources, or require resources for technological equipment. Resources are cited for those programs.

The Winners

The Top Five Programs

Albany Public Library New Scotland Branch, Albany, New York: Skateboarding Discussion Group

Austin Public Library, Austin, Texas: Second Chance Books

Cleveland Public Library, Cleveland, Ohio: Teen Empowerment: A Motivational Summit (T.E.A.M.S.)

Hennepin County Library, Minnetonka, Minnesota: International Teen Club

Alameda County Library, Fremont, California: Teen/Senior Web Connection

The "Best of the Rest"

Monroe County (New York) Library System, Fairport Library Council and Fairport Central School District: Greater Rochester Teen Book Festival

Loudoun County (Virginia.) Public Library: Hanging Out Rocks!

Homer (Illinois) Public Library District: Energy: A Teen Leadership Academy

Louisville (Kentucky) Free Public Library: Anime Con

Cheshire (Connecticut) Public Library: Teen Podcast

Randolph County (North Carolina.) Public Library: Teen Corner @ your library

Seward Park Branch, New York Public Library: Teen Advisory Group Garden

West Covina Library, County of Los Angeles Library System: Cultural Heritage Series for Young Adults

Virginia School for the Deaf and the Blind, Blind Department, Staunton: ABC Café Audiobook Club

Fairfield Civic Center Branch of the Solano County (California) Library: Teenie Boppers

Berkeley (California) Public Library: Vera Casey Parenting Class

Prince George's County (Maryland) Memorial Library System: Outreach to the Crossroads Youth Opportunity Center

Alachua County (Florida) Library District: Teen Artist of the Month

The New York Public Library: Classic Literature for Teenagers

Donnell Library Center, New York Public Library: Anti-Prom

San José (California) Public Library: San José Teen Idol

Livermore (California) Public Library: Teen Film Festival: An Independent View

East Jessamine (Kentucky) Middle School: Student Novel Nibbles Party

Deltona Regional Library, Volusia County, Florida:. The X-Room

Monroe County (Michigan) Library System: 2007: Year of the Teen

The Excellence in Library Service to Young Adults Project was started by ALA Past President Hardy Franklin in 1993. All five rounds of the project have been funded by the Margaret Alexander Edwards Trust. Edwards was a well-known and innovative young adult services librarian at Enoch Pratt Free Library in Baltimore, Maryland, for more than thirty years. (See Appendix D, "About Margaret A. Edwards.")

one

Enhancing Teen Spaces, Physical or Virtual

The description for this category included teen space makeovers, Web-based services, or programs for teens or projects that make libraries in schools and public sectors more teen friendly or accessible. Not every school or public library has large designated pleasure reading or visiting space for teens, but many libraries find ways to honor teen needs and interests physically or online.

TITLE OF THE PROGRAM/SERVICE

Teen Artist of the Month

Alachua County Library District, Gainesville, Florida

Type of program/service:
Series/ongoing program/service

Targeted audiences:
Middle School, Junior High, Senior High

Name of contact person:
Diane Colson, dcolson@aclib.us

Other categories for this program:
Community Connections, Special Events

Program Summary

In 2005, the youth services department decided to hold a teen art contest in celebration of Teen Read Week™. The response was very positive, with many area teens submitting their original artwork. The winning artwork was displayed on the walls of the young adult area of the headquarters branch. After this success, the library staff repeated the teen art contest for Teen Read Week 2006. More than one hundred pieces of artwork were submitted for the contest, with more than forty teen artists competing. The winning artwork enhanced the attractiveness of the area so much that staff decided to display the artwork of local teens all year long. This led to the inception of the Teen Artist of the Month program, which officially began in February 2007. Any teen can sign up to have their artwork displayed in the young adult area for an entire month. In May 2007, the library staff already had a teen artist scheduled for each month through March 2008.

Steps

The Teen Artist of the Month program is advertised on the library district Web site and through flyers distributed at the ten branches. The flyer simply states, "Calling All Teen Artists," and gives a brief description of the parameters and who to contact.

The library staff maintains a sign-up sheet for interested artists, assigning them a month as soon as staff determines they are eligible. This gives most of them plenty of time to plan, as the program is booked for about nine months in advance.

Approximately ten days before the next artist will have their work displayed, the library staff contact them. Their parents need to sign a release form for the artwork. They drop it off at the library before the next month begins.

The library staff takes down the old artwork and hangs up the new. It generally takes about two hours to do this, depending on the number of pieces. The teens are then contacted to pick up their artwork at the library.

Description of Library

The Alachua County Library District is located in North Central Florida. There are ten branches and two bookmobiles to serve the Alachua County population. The library district offers library cards to any resident in Florida, so the library also serves many of the contiguous counties on a regular basis. The largest city in Alachua County is Gainesville, home of the University of Florida. The influence of the university is certainly strong in the library district, creating a culturally diverse population. The headquarters branch is located in the heart of downtown Gainesville. Most of Gainesville's African American population lives in the immediate area surrounding the headquarters branch. This is where the youth services department, which includes the young adult area mentioned in this application, is located.

Intended Audience and Demographics

The Teen Artist of the Month is intended for Alachua County residents between the ages of 12 and 18. There are approximately 15,152 students enrolled in the middle and high schools of Alachua County. About 20 percent of the population of Alachua County is African American, 6.4 percent is Hispanic, and 67.9 percent is white. The adolescent population surrounding the headquarters branch is predominately African American, with many teens living close enough to walk to the library. Many of these teens come on a regular basis to use the computers.

Rationale

The library district has long fostered relationships with the teens in Alachua County, with a primary focus on books and reading. Library staff regularly visit area schools for booktalks, produce booklists for teens, and strive to select literature that will entice readers at all levels of proficiency. But the library staff wanted to establish a sense of personal connection between the teens in the community and the physical space of the library. The library staff started the teen art contest as a way to see if any teens would be interested in seeing their artwork prominently displayed in a public place, and the library staff has been rewarded by the enthusiastic response. Many teens brought family, friends, and classmates to see their exhibits. They were obviously very proud that their creations were deemed worthy enough for display. The artwork forged a connection between individual teens and the institution of the library, creating not only a more beautiful area for the teens but establishing their importance as contributors to the community at large.

Numbers of Young Adults Reached

The Teen Artist of the Month program has sixteen artists currently signed up to display their work. A more accurate gauge of the reach of the program, however, is in response to the teen art contest of October 2006, which prompted the inception of the Teen Artist of the Month. There were more than forty teen artists who submitted work for that contest.

Numbers of Staff and Volunteers

Two staff members, a librarian and a library specialist, from the youth services department work with maintaining contacts with the teens and managing the logistics of hanging the artwork. They also designed and printed the flyers advertising the program, using the office printer. The public relations specialist contacted the local newspaper for publicity, and the library staff posted a notice, "Calling All Teen Artists" on the Web page.

To set up the program, a library specialist designed the flyer. This took her about four hours. The graphic designer (administrative assistant) spent about three hours preparing this for the Web site and making a template for small flyers to be distributed to the branches. The public relations specialist (another adminstrative assistant) took about three hours to contact local newspapers, including an entry on a blog offered by the *Gainesville Voice*.

The continuance of the program is maintained by a librarian/library specialist team. These two are responsible for contacting the artists, receiving their work, and hanging the artwork in the young adult area. This usually amounts to only about four hours of work per month.

Funding and Budget Figures

There was no outside funding for the program. All costs are calculated in terms of library staff hours and materials such as paper for publicity flyers and hardware for hanging the artwork. Here is a breakdown of expenditures:

Initial setup of program

Library specialist (flyers)		
	4 hours @ $12.27	$49.08
Administrative assistant		
	6 hours @ $15.43	$92.58
Paper cost		$16.32

Monthly cost to maintain display

Librarian		
	2 hours @ $17.26	$34.52
Library specialist		
	2 hours @ $12.27	$24.54
Materials for hanging art		$10.00
	TOTAL	$227.04

Marketing

The main area newspaper, the *Gainesville Sun*, included the Teen Artist of the Month as one of its "Best Bets for Kids." One of the smaller newspapers, the *Gainesville Voice*, ran an article about the first teen artist to display her work in February 2007. This article included a photo of the girl holding her artwork while standing in front of the display in the library. For the month of February, the library staff posted an advertisement on the home Web page entitled, "Calling All Teen Artists" that gave information about signing up for the program. The library staff also printed small flyers to distribute from each of the ten library branches calling for participants.

Youth Participation

The bulk of labor involved in Teen Artist of the Month is the creation of the artwork, which is done exclusively by the teens. The teens are also responsible for selecting which pieces they would like to display and for providing cards with the title of the piece and any other information of interest that they would like to share with the public. The Youth Services Department is the only the facilitator of the program, responsible for publicity and the actual hanging of the artwork. In terms of evaluation, the response of local teens to the call for teen artists was greater than the total attendance of all of the in-house young adult programs for 2006.

Evaluation

The program can be evaluated in several ways. One is that the library did receive a large response from teen artists in the community. The Teen Artist of the Month display has also brought more visitors to the headquarters branch library, because two of the artists brought their school classes to

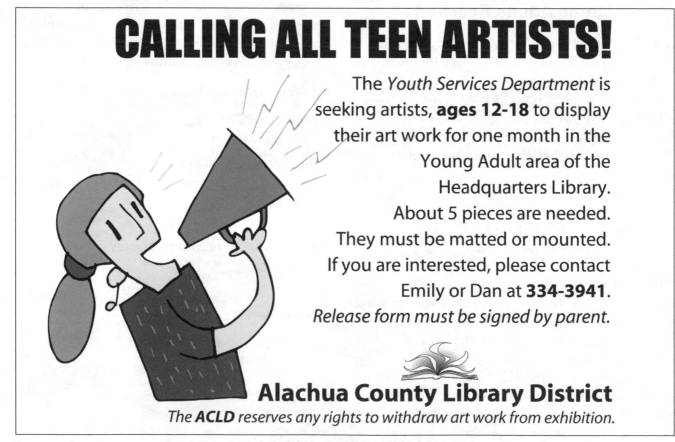

An ad from the library Web site

view the exhibits. This resulted in a measurable increase of forty-six more patrons. There have probably been more visitors to the art exhibit that have escaped the count. And the young adult area has definitely improved its appearance, with one large wall that was formerly empty now graced with the color and creativity of teen art.

This initiative has made a big difference in the young adult area, giving it an authentic teen feel. The teens who participate are very proud to have their work displayed so prominently. They bring in friends and family, and in the two cases mentioned previously, whole classes to see the display. Library staff is spared the work of creating attractive materials to decorate the young adult area and the teen art is more imaginative and relevant than anything the library could produce. The fact that the display changes each month means that the area is always getting a fresh look, with minimal effort.

Good record-keeping is essential. The teens would be very disappointed if somehow they missed their chance to display their artwork. It helps to see the artwork a few days before the actual hanging, just in case something is inappropriate. The library staff asked the teens themselves to prepare cards with their names and the titles of each piece that the library staff hang with the artwork, which helps answer queries from interested patrons.

Suggested Variations

The library staff has allocated one large wall to the Teen Artist of the Month, with shelf space on top of the bookcases in the young adult area for three-dimensional work. This could include mobiles, if your space allows. Other possible places to display artwork might be hallways and pillars. Other libraries could consider devoting bulletin board space to teen artwork. The display time could be varied as well, especially if your library is not open year-round. The teens themselves could be responsible for organizing the art display.

Relevance to Overall Young Adult Services at Institution

The youth services department strives to entice teens to come into the library "by hook or by crook." Teens may not think of themselves as potential library users simply because they have never entered the building. The Teen Artist of the Month appeals to teens who may not be big readers or who have not had any previous encounters with the library district, but who have a desire to create art. The library staff does not judge the merits of the artwork, as the library staff did with the teen art contest, before they hang it on display. Any teen who would like to participate is allowed to have their assigned month. This creates a new opportunity for teens to feel included in the library and the community.

Teen Podcast Program

Cheshire Public Library, Cheshire, Connecticut

Type of the program/service:
Series/ongoing program/service

Targeted audience:
Senior High

Name of contact person:
Sarah Kline Morgan
smorgan@cheshirelibrary.org

Other Categories for this program:
Creative Teen Clubs

Program Summary

The Cheshire Public Library's (CPL) Teen Podcast program is the brainchild of Sarah Kline Morgan, CPL's teen services librarian. Launched in early 2006, this online audio-cultural magazine, produced exclusively by teens in grades 9 through 12, features book and music reviews, readings of original literature, and much more. The podcast provides a creative outlet to Cheshire's teens by allowing them to express themselves in a contemporary medium that is attractive to their age group. Using a microphone, an Apple computer, and GarageBand software, Cheshire teens regularly plan, record, edit, and upload a half-hour audio variety show, which is then available to listeners worldwide through Apple's iTunes Store, streaming through the library's Web site, or burned to CD.

ent scout and work to identify a few teens with the creative energy and technical expertise necessary to excel in leadership roles. Teachers and school media specialists can be good people to talk to for references, especially advisers to extracurricular programs like the drama club or the literary magazine. Outreach visits to these clubs are also a useful tool for recruitment. The CPL Podcast became a reality when one enthusiastic student, approached about the project, expressed his enthusiasm and asked for a management role. This led to the creation of an executive body, the editorial board, made up of students with the greatest stake in the project, committed to participate on an ongoing basis. Once a few teens signed on, their involvement spurred further involvement. A few enthusiastic participants can quickly blossom into a thriving group.

Steps

Recruitment

Recruitment isn't an obvious first step, but it is crucial for a program that relies heavily on teen leadership. The librarian must think like a tal-

Equipment

Decisions regarding the purchase of equipment are best made in conjunction with teens, if possible. Equipment required for startup is very minimal: a computer, editing software, and a microphone.

Training

Most teens will need limited training in the skills necessary to create and edit a podcast, but a baseline training session is a good idea. Once a few teens are trained to use the computer and the software, they can then teach future participants. The CPL Podcast has a few teens that are particularly adept with the recording setup, and these teens make themselves available to help freelancers who may not have the time or inclination to learn the system themselves.

Developing a Schedule and Format

Like any publication—print or multimedia—a podcast has a production schedule. In conjunction with the librarian, teens need to decide on the length of episodes and how often to release them. A production schedule can be adjusted. Teens should also decide on the parameters for content. Some teen library podcasts are completely library-related, others are review-based, and others, like that of CPL, are variety shows featuring a broad range of original teen content.

Recording, Editing, and Releasing

Once a production schedule has been determined, the next step is to schedule recording sessions for the contributors. The CPL Podcast is hosted by a teen who provides transitions between the segments. The production schedule includes individual recording sessions at the participants' convenience, and a scheduled group recording session is followed by time for the host to record transitions. Editing happens during recording sessions for many of the contributors, but editing after the fact is also done by teens with particular aptitude and by the teen librarian. For the CPL Podcast the teen librarian, who must sign off on the content before it is released, does the final listen-through, edit, and upload. For security reasons, teen podcasters do not participate in the upload process.

Description of Library

The Cheshire Public Library serves a population of 29,000 residents in a suburban New England environment. The library's annual circulation is approximately 390,000 items, or more than 13 items per capita. In late 2005, the library completed its first-ever strategic planning process using *The New Planning For Results: A Streamlined Approach* by Sandra Nelson (ALA 2001) as a guide. Key to the CPL Strategic Plan is a focus on services to children, teens, and families. Since implementing the strategic plan in 2006, funding and support for collections and services for youth have been increased, resulting in much higher circulation of youth materials and increased attendance at programs.

Intended Audience and Demographics

The intended audience for CPL's Teen Podcast is students in grades 9 through 12. Circulation of items in the teen collection is very high, but because local teens tend to be very involved, driven, young people, it is difficult to keep them at the library for programs, considering the many activities and projects with which the library has to compete, such as school, test preparation, sports, music lessons, and more.

Rationale

Cheshire's youth are savvy and the library had been having a hard time keeping them interested in using the library's programs and services. Circulation and attendance figures were stagnant, and there was very little interest or involvement on the part of Cheshire's teens. In fact, yearly circulation of teen books and materials was hovering around a mere 5,000 items, or about 1.4 percent of the library's total circulation.

In August 2005, the Cheshire Public Library welcomed Sarah Kline Morgan as its full-time teen services librarian. It soon became apparent that not only did Morgan have great ideas about what kinds of programs would bring teens into the library, but that she had the organizational skills and the drive to make those programs come to fruition. In just a few months, Sarah drummed up interest in several new CPL teen programs, such as a Teen Book Board, a teen book blog, and of course, the Teen Podcast.

In early 2006, podcasting was still considered a "fringe" technology, and it certainly was not used widely in public libraries. However, Morgan saw the potential for attracting teens to the library through podcasting and she quickly developed a core podcasting team. Some of the students were regular library users, but others rarely, if ever, used the library. Word of mouth spread quickly, and soon there was a large slate of students eager to contribute their skills and precious time to the podcast. Some had computer or audio editing skills and were willing to provide a technical-support role to the project. Others were more interested in the performance or literary aspects, so these students became writers or hosts of podcast segments, which frequently include original literature or poetry readings, "The Love/Hate Music Debate," and more.

The CPL Teen Podcast makes a difference in the lives of Cheshire's young adults by creating a partnership between teens and their library. The emphasis that the library places on empowering the teens to do as much of the planning and execution of the program as possible is the core of the program. Strict oversight, too many rules, and a generally "institutional" atmosphere would have been disastrous to this program, and so they were avoided, resulting in tremendously positive outcomes. The podcast also develops technical knowledge, fosters creative expression, and promotes the growth of leadership skills. The library now has a growing loyal constituency of teens who are active and engaged in library programs and services. One teen member of the podcast editorial board said:

> I've been waiting for something like this my whole life. It's something new, something interesting, something that gets a lot of people involved.

Recently the library staff has been pleased to note that many more young people are expressing an interest in working as pages at CPL, which bodes well for the future of the library and for the profession of librarianship in general—many current librarians started out as pages! The library staff has even had to step up its teen volunteer program to handle the surge in interest in the library. Another added bonus for the teen podcasters is that several of them have prominently featured their podcast activities on college applications.

Numbers of Young Adults Reached

There is a core of about a dozen regular or freelance teen contributors to the podcast. Through downloads streaming via the Web site or episodes burned to CD, thousands of listeners have enjoyed the CPL Teen Podcast.

Numbers of Staff and Volunteers

There is one full-time staff member involved in this project—Morgan, the teen services librarian. All other contributors are teens involved in the production of the project.

Funding and Budget Figures

The project was funded from the teen programming budget, which comes exclusively from the Friends of the Cheshire Public Library. It is a very inexpensive program to produce because the equipment involved includes an Apple computer and its included GarageBand software, both of which the library already owned, but which could be purchased new for less than $1,500.

The library also purchased a high-quality microphone for approximately $125. Flyers are reproduced in-house for a few cents each. Staff time, at approximately $24 per hour, is minimal; aside from a bit of oversight as to the content and technical aspects of the program, the teen podcasters really run the show. In total, the teen services librarian averages about one hour per week on the podcast.

Marketing

Marketing was done primarily through word of mouth by students. Morgan quickly built a rapport with teens early in her tenure at CPL, and the podcast was such an intriguing and innovative program that word quickly spread. However, the library staff also printed flyers, advertised the program on the Web site, and sent press releases to the local news media, which resulted in extensive coverage of the podcast.

The CPL Teen Podcast was publicly recognized by teen library services expert Patrick Jones at a Public Library Association workshop in Boston in 2006. National press includes articles or mentions in *VOYA* (Dec. 2006), *School Library Journal* (Jan. 10, 2006), and *American Libraries* (March 2007). Most notably, the CPL Teen Podcast was the recipient of the Connecticut Excellence in Public Library Service Award for 2007.

Youth Participation

The Teen Podcast is a teen-driven cultural magazine featuring teen writers, musicians, commentators, reviewers, and more. There is an extremely high level of youth participation in planning, implementing, and evaluating the podcast. In fact, all podcast segments are conceived, planned, written, recorded, edited, and uploaded by the teen podcasters, with assistance from the teen librarian. Participation in the podcast is limited to high school students. The podcast incorporates other CPL teen programs, including the

Teen Book Board, whose members provide book reviews. Shows are ten to twenty minutes long and are released every two to four weeks during the academic year. All content is original. Listeners have several options: they can use the iTunes Store to subscribe to the podcast, go to the library Web site to listen in streaming audio, or pick up CD copies of each episode in the library teen area.

Evaluation

The program has been evaluated by participation, output, and usage statistics. Thirteen podcast episodes have been released over the course of the project, an average of one episode per month. The podcast has been downloaded from Apple iTunes a total of 2,091 times. An unknown number of users have listened to the podcast via the streaming audio link from the Cheshire Public Library's Web site, and dozens of copies of the podcast burned to CD have been distributed. Teen circulation, which hovered around 5,000 items annually as recently as 2005, exceeded 13,000 items in fiscal year 2007, an increase of more than 250 percent in the course of just one year.

The CPL Teen Podcast is an ongoing program, so staff has had opportunities to adjust approaches over time. When the CPL Teen Podcast began in January 2006, podcasts were not very popular in the community. This continues to be an ongoing challenge for the program. Recruitment of both participants and listeners is hard when so many people, including teens, are unfamiliar with podcasting. Staff began to think of the program as a creative program rather than a technology program, and then began to focus the marketing accordingly to emphasize content, rather than technology. Potential listeners and contributors are drawn in by the quality of the content, and adapt to the technology as necessary.

In the beginning, staff thought of the podcast like a radio show, and so it began with thirty-minute episodes, which were much too long. After four episodes, the length was cut back to ten to twenty minutes. Longer episodes pose problems both from a production perspective and for listeners who are frustrated by long download times. Coordinating recording sessions gets more difficult as more segments are added per episode, and the editing gets exponentially more complicated. After a few catastrophic editing experiences where files were lost or corrupted and deadlines missed, staff talked to listeners to learn their preferences.

Suggested Variations

Teen podcasting has endless variations. In the medium-sized Chesire Public Library, staff has the resources, staff time, and teen interest to support an ongoing variety show with regularly released episodes. Less intensive models for teen podcasts might include irregular episodes produced during specially scheduled programs, designed around certain themes, or person-on-the-street style interviews conducted by the teen librarian or library director. Traditional library services like readers' advisory and instruction can be adapted for podcast episodes. Podcasts featuring one-shot book reviews, for instance, are a natural fit for libraries, as are library tours or mini-lessons. Teens are drawn to podcasts produced by teens rather than adults.

Relevance to Overall Young Adult Services at Institution

The podcast is the keystone of teen services at the Cheshire Public Library. It's the program that has received the most publicity and interest from Cheshire's teens. It has been extraordinarily successful in attracting new teen users to the library through its reputation as a great creative outlet, where teens have free reign (with only the necessary minimal oversight by library staff). The goal, when providing services to Cheshire's teens, is to create lifelong readers and library users and supporters. Today's teens are viewed as tomorrow's community leaders. By ensuring their involvement and interest in the library today, a vibrant and relevant future for the library is guaranteed.

Resources

Making a Podcast with FeedBurner and Blogger: www.podcastingnews.com/articles/Make_ Podcast_Blogger.html

Blogger: www.blogger.com/home

Podcasts and FeedBurner: www.feedburner.com/ fb/a/podcasts

Making a podcast (from iTunes): www.apple.com/ itunes/store/podcaststechspecs.html

Podcasting with Teens (from YALSA): www.ala .org/ala/yalsa/teentechweek/ttw08/resources abcd/techguide_podcast.pdf

Teen Advisory Group Garden

Seward Park Branch Library, New York Public Library

Type of program/service:
Series/ongoing program/service

Targeted audiences:
Middle School, Junior High, Senior High

Name of contact person:
Sarah Couri, scouri@nypl.org

Other categories for this program:
Creative Teen Clubs

Program Summary

The Seward Park Teen Advisory Group (TAG) meets weekly. The group discusses a wide variety of topics and works on many teen-initiated projects. One such project began when the teens expressed an interest in creating a garden. They decided to make a container garden on a concrete square in a fenced-in area near the street. Working with a local artist, P. Oliver, they planned the strategy and came up with a timeline. The TAG and staff decided that the artist would meet with the group for five sessions to work with clay to make planters. The teens shaped and painted the planters, and then worked to prime and paint the cinderblocks to personalize the space. Staff worked with a mixture of city agencies and local businesses to make the garden.

Description of Library

The Seward Park Branch is located in the Lower East Side of New York City, on the edge of Chinatown. This is one branch of the New York Public Library, an eighty-five-branch system that serves a diverse city. The teen area serves a very active population, defined as ages 12 to 18,

housing a sizable collection of books and graphic novels (more than 8,000 titles in English, Chinese, and Spanish) for leisure reading, homework assistance, and guidance for college and careers, along with magazines and CDs. The teen section resides on the third floor of Seward Park, alongside the reference collection, the CD collection, and the adult nonfiction collection. The library offers four Internet computers for teen use. Although the teen area is not physically separated from the rest of the floor, teens have claimed one corner of the room, visually marking it with two large bulletin boards and two tables for teen use.

Intended Audience and Demographics

Of New York City's 8.1 million residents, nearly one-quarter are under the age of 18. Almost 850,000 are between the ages of 10 and 18. New York City teens are very diverse. A great percentage of these young adults are immigrants. Teens on New York's Lower East Side number about 12,000. More than 36 percent of families with children under 18 live below the poverty level in the neighborhood of this branch. The teens who use the library are very active users; they come in regularly. Many of these teens find themselves spending afternoons at the library, using computers and reading graphic novels.

The teens at Seward Park live or go to school in the neighborhood (there are six high schools and four middle schools in the few blocks surrounding Seward Park). There is a large ESL population in this area as well. Many of the teens are bi- and trilingual, speaking combinations of Mandarin, Cantonese, Fujianese, Spanish, and English. The young adults find empowerment at the library through the TAG. Many teens at Seward Park have grown up translating for parents and grandparents. They now speak up for themselves and their own needs on Friday afternoons at the TAG.

Numbers of Young Adults Reached

The Seward Park TAG is a group of about thirty teens. On average, twenty teens attend TAG meetings each week. The group spent nearly sixty hours engaged in research and planning the garden. Additionally, this same group of teens spent more than twenty hours working to make the garden a reality by painting, sculpting, and planting. And they continue to work on it.

Number of Staff and Volunteers

The Seward Park staff has also helped with the TAG Garden. One staff member was a botany minor in college, and she advised the TAG on plants and how to care for the garden. The entire staff sat in on meetings at one time or another to witness the progress of the garden. They have even expressed interest in painting one of the cinderblocks. The project is uniting the staff as well as the teens.

Some city agencies helped this initiative. The New York City Arbor Day Committee gives out free trees each year to organizations that work with youth. The TAG applied for a tree, and as a result, the garden houses a young serviceberry tree. The New York City Department of Parks and Recreation also helped with the project. The Manhattan Forestry Department has generously agreed to provide a planter made from recycled trees.

Funding and Budget Figures

The TAG Garden has a budget of $2,500, provided by the Cultural After School Adventure Program by New York City Council Member Rosie Mendez and the City of New York. This has covered the cost of the garden materials, including paint, clay, and plants. A local business, Schames and Son Paint, has also generously donated paint. P. Oliver donated twenty cinderblocks, which are used for various garden structures, including planter stands and benches, and offered to donate one free session so that the teens can work with clay to make something for themselves to take home.

Youth Participation

All of the work, from gardening research to picking out paint to helping protect the plants from squirrels and other hungry critters, has been performed by teens. Coordinated by the single young adult librarian, and working closely with P. Oliver, the teens have pulled together to spearhead this venture. They created the planters, sculpting and painting them in a five-session series. They cleaned, primed, and painted the twenty cinderblocks, fashioning intricate and beautiful designs and pictures. They picked various books as inspiration for their cinderblock art—from *Blood Song* by Eric Drooker to pictures inspired by anime and manga. They work to arrange the plants in the garden, basing it on attractiveness as well as practicality.

Marketing

This program has been advertised on the library's Web site, and flyers were distributed among teens and at schools. However, the strongest advertising has come from the teens themselves; their word of mouth has spread, and new teens come to each session, wanting to contribute their time and attention to the garden. It's a real tribute to the success of the program that attendance grows at each session, and that the teens keep returning for hard work and creative fun.

Evaluation

The TAG Garden has been an overwhelming success already. The TAG has even bigger plans for the future, including painting a mural on the cement under the garden to further mark the space. The group would like to use the garden to host their own meetings and have garden parties to celebrate it. It has been an unexpected source of pro-teen publicity as well. Each day while working outside, countless people walk by, impressed by the dedication and creativity that the teens are pouring into the space. The TAG Garden is a constant reminder of the potential power and energy that teens wield.

Working outside in the garden area was absolutely the most satisfying part for the teens. They found planting and nurturing the new garden to be an incredible experience. Many teens came to their first TAG meeting only because they got to "dig around in dirt." Painting the cinderblocks also happened outside and was a phenomenal experience. Since they came up with such amazing designs and gorgeous pictures, the staff was then able to secure permission to paint a mural on the garden sidewalk.

Changes to this program would have included using the money or asking for donations to buy a few large-sized planters. The cinderblocks would work better as stands rather than planters.

Suggested Variations

Other libraries could invite their teen groups to build an indoor garden or a rooftop garden. They could also team up with a local park or gardening group to create a space outside of library property. Teens could plant a tree to begin an environmental discussion.

Relevance to
Overall Young Adult Services

As mentioned in the marketing section, working outside was a boon for pro-teen publicity at Seward Park. Many passersby stopped, captivated at the sight of groups of dedicated teens working hard to create a beautiful space. They asked questions and complimented the teens' obvious dedication and creativity. It was an opportunity to remind the community just how much teens contribute to the library and to the greater community.

One of the TAG's goals is to help teens find their role in their local community, and find their voices in their lives. All the chosen projects are teen-driven initiatives; they come up with the project and then work to see the project through to its completion. The TAG Garden exemplifies these goals. The TAG noticed that the recently renovated branch needed beautifying outside as well as inside. City teens do not often get a chance to get outside and study nature up close. The teens at Seward Park were immediately enthusiastic about this concept. As a society, as concerns about the environment grow, this project has been instrumental in showing Seward Park teens that they might have some of the answers.

Before the teens began working in the garden area, it was completely empty and used only as a garbage dump (bags of library trash and recycling waited there for garbage day). Now, the five hundred square foot area is being put to beautiful use; teens marked the outside of the library as their own, and reclaimed an urban area for nature.

Teen Corner @ your library®

Randolph County Public Library, Asheboro, North Carolina

Type of program/service:
Series/ongoing program/service

Targeted audiences:
Middle School, Junior High, Senior High

Name of contact person:
Amy Keith Barney,
akeith@randolphlibrary.org

Program Summary

The radical transformation of the staid library headquarter's young adult collection into the vibrant Teen Corner has set the tone for an equally radical redesign of the library's approach to teen services. The makeover included a bold paint job to distinguish the corner from the rest of the library; new seating; high-end computers offering project software such as video/audio editing; contemporary display islands for graphic novels, magazines, and featured books; as well as artwork and posters.

The project, which kicked off on February 24, 2007, with a local teen rock band playing in the library, anchors a marketing campaign that has included creation of a teen logo, a teen-branded library card, teen-oriented graphics, a full-color teen newsletter, a teen summer reading program, monthly programming, and a Teen Advisory Board. The project already has shown a significant increase in the number of teen cardholders, and a jump in circulation of material to teens. Between the February 2007 kickoff and the end of September 2007, the number of new teen cardholders increased 73 percent over the same period the previous year, compared to a 15 percent increase overall among all library patrons.

The circulation of material to teens increased 34 percent, compared to a 4 percent increase overall.

Steps

In developing the project, library staff and volunteers:

- Collaborated with a library school student on a survey of teen library users.
- Created a marketing plan for teen services as part of a multisession marketing workshop offered by the State Library of North Carolina.
- Applied for and received an Library Services and Technology Act (LSTA) Marketing Grant administered by the State Library of North Carolina to fund:
  - the creation of a teen services logo and specialized graphics;
  - the creation of teen promotional material with logo and graphics, including a teen-branded library card, registration kits (bags, bookmarks, welcome brochures), posters, and banners;

- ALA and other promotional material aimed at teens; and
- the creation and publication of teen newsletter.
- Formed staff committee to manage Teen Corner project.
- Solicited library foundation for funds to furnish revamped teen area.
- Sought and obtained deep discount from furniture manufacturer for eight tablet-arm upholstered chairs.
- Purchased modern steel display islands and Caper task chairs.
- Sought and received voluntary assistance from local interior designer for Teen Corner arrangement, colors, and so on.
- Formed the Teen Advisory Board consisting of teen volunteers who meet monthly to gain input on Teen Corner design and teen programming.
- Brought in former state library youth services consultant to present development workshop on working with teens for all staff.
- Commissioned logo design and graphics from area comic book artist. (With logo and graphics in hand, created teen library card, welcome brochure, bookmarks, bags, and banners).
- Solicited and received funds from Friends of the Library for Teen Corner embellishments such as paint, wallpaper, decal work, and commissioned artwork.
- Worked with county maintenance staff, contractors, interior designer and others, to renovate the headquarters library Teen Corner.
- With Teen Advisory Board, staff and Friends of the Library, planned and carried out a kickoff day featuring a local teen rock band, Mexican folk dancers, and a pizza lunch.
- Began issuing teen cards to anyone age 13 to18 who was registering for a library card,

and trading teen cards for regular library cards for those in the age group who already were library patrons.
- Began publication of full-color monthly teen newsletter.
- Began monthly teen programming.

Description of Library

The Randolph County Public Library serves 135,000 people in Randolph County, North Carolina, and more in the surrounding area. The library system, a county government agency, includes seven community libraries and is headquartered at the Asheboro Public Library. The library system has more than 70,000 cardholders, recorded 376,373 visits in 2005–2006, circulated 413,892 items, and recorded more than 100,000 Internet uses. Strongly tied to their communities, in 2006 and 2007, the libraries hosted 157 programs for adults drawing more than 3,300 attendees, and 951 children's programs drawing 28,808 attendees.

The library's mission is: "to provide the reading and informational needs of the citizens of Randolph and surrounding counties." One of its seven general objectives is: "to provide opportunity and encouragement for children, young people, men and women to educate themselves continuously," and it was with this objective in mind that the Teen Corner project was undertaken.

Intended Audience and Demographics

Until the Teen Corner project, there was no outreach to teens beyond the ongoing development of a young adult collection. According to 2000 census data, there were 17,477 teens in Randolph County. Although 52 percent of county residents were library cardholders, only about 27 percent of teens had library cards. Nevertheless, circulation of teen material had increased by 26 percent over five years, while overall circulation of materials in the library decreased slightly.

randolph county
public library
www.randolphlibrary.org

news

The very best place to start.

Volume XV No. 8   •   February 2007

Hang out at 'The Corner'
Live band, pizza to kick off revamped teen area

♣ The Asheboro library will introduce its redesigned area for teens with a kick-off featuring performances by local rock band Bantum Rooster with guest Brittnee Loflin, and the dance troupe Grupo Folklórico Guadalupano, 11 a.m.-4 p.m. Saturday, February 24.

Bantum Rooster — Doyle Hinkle, Christian Morgan and Shane Morgan, with guest star Brittnee Loflin — will perform for the kickoff of The Corner, 11 a.m.-4 p.m. Saturday, February 24, at the Asheboro library. Find out more about the band at www.myspace.com/bantumrooster.

This event will be LOUD!

At lunchtime, pizza will be served for teens ages 13-18. The kickoff, hosted by the library's Teen Advisory Board (TAB), is free and the public is invited.

The new teen-focused area, called 'The Corner' because it keys off of the alcove that houses part of the library's teen-oriented collection of books, magazines, comic books and graphic novels, includes:

• Eight new armchairs with tablet writing surfaces purchased from Jack Cartwright Inc. of High Point;
• Steel display islands for magazines, graphic novels, and featured books, DVDs and music;
• Four new computers featuring Word, PowerPoint, Publisher and Excel plus video editing software and

access to research databases such as NC LIVE;
• A new color scheme, and a logo designed by graphic artist Brian Shearer, to set the area apart;
• Bright banners, posters and displays promoting library services to teens and featuring material of interest to teens.

The kick-off also will inaugurate ongoing promotions and programming directed at teens, including a flashy new library card, a quarterly newsletter, monthly programs organized by the TAB, and a teen Summer Reading Program .

The new emphasis on library services to teens is made possible by multiple funding sources see *From the Director* on page 2 for more.

Trade your library card!

If you're in middle or high school, trade in your old library card for the new teen-branded card, FREE! Ask about your new card at your local library checkout desk; new cards will be available beginning February 24.

Williams' arrowhead display to return March 3

The arrowhead and American Indian artifact collection of Warner Williams — regarded as one of the best anywhere — will be on display all day Saturday, March 3 (ONE DAY ONLY this year), at the Asheboro library. Williams will be on hand to answer questions.

The library newsletter features Teen Corner.

PROMOTIONAL MATERIAL

Provided by a Library Services and Technology Act grant administered by the State Library of North Carolina, Department of Cultural Resources.

Teen Advisory Board (TAB) members, in TAB t-shirts provided by the Friends of the Library, trade their old library cards for new teen cards.

Teen Library Card!
Logo designed by Brian Shearer, www.gravyboy.com

Welcome Kit
For new teen library card recipients

Banners
2'x3'; 3'x6' (more are in the works!)

Get Creative on these computers:
- Video/Audio/Photo Editing
- Research Databases
- PowerPoint
- Word
- Excel
- Access
- And More!

LOGIN WITH YOUR LIBRARY CARD

Read
The Teen Corner includes all this and more:
- New Teen Fiction
- Graphic Novels
- Magazines
- Comics
- Wireless Internet Access

Randolph County Public Library's
Smartest Card
Get it. Use it.
@ your library
www.randolphlibrary.org

Randolph County Public Library
Teen Corner

www.randolphlibrary.org/teens.html
rcplteencorner.blogspot.com
myspace.com/rcplteencorner

Teen Newsletter
In print and online

Flyers and other promotional tools for Teen Corner

17

TEEN PROGRAMMING

Teen Corner Kickoff

Bantum Rooster with guest Britnee Loflin rocks the library; door prizes; pizza is served; Grupo Folklórico Guadalupano performs folk dances!

Recent and Upcoming...

February
Genealogy For Teens
Teen Corner Kickoff
March
Video Editing for Teens
April
Book Swap for Teens
College 101: Strategies for First Year Success
June (Teen Summer Reading — various branches)
Game Day (board games, cards, trivia)
College 101
Get Blogging
Clueless
Page Turners
July (Teen Summer Reading — various branches)
Unlocking the Past
Origami
Slices & Sleuths Teen Pizza Party
Scavenger Hunt and Wrap-up Party

video editing for teens
@ 4:30 p.m.
thursday, march 22
edit video clips and make them into movies free and all teens are invited!

COLLEGE 101
strategies for 1st year success

Randolph County Public Library
Teen Corner

www.randolphlibrary.org/teens.html
rcplteencorner.blogspot.com
myspace.com/rcplteencorner

Another flyer advertising Teen Corner

These disparities led library staff to conclude that there was an untapped market among local teenagers who would find the library relevant if they knew about opportunities for teens at the library. In 2005 and early 2006, two reference staff members initiated a teen blog, and obtained Friends of the Library sponsorship for a series of successful teen-oriented programs including poetry open mic nights; a Harry Potter book discussion; and covering popular topics such as blogging, comics, and graphic novels. Participation by staff in a series of State Library of North Carolina marketing workshops led to a teen-focused LSTA marketing grant and the Teen Corner project.

Rationale

The Teen Corner project has proven important in three respects. First, teens in the community appreciate it immensely and are being drawn to the library by it. Second, it has shown the library how to reach teens in a way it was not reaching them before. And finally, it has raised the profile of the library in the community, inspiring a new level of cooperation with school media coordinators and generating support among parents.

In a survey of teen library users taken prior to the project, respondents overwhelmingly stated that, in the words of one, "some cool furniture and a lounge area would be great."

This sentiment was borne out shortly after the Teen Corner debuted when a young athlete told us how much she appreciated doing her homework in the comfortable new tablet arm chairs after soccer practice. On Valentine's Day, a teen couple secluded themselves in the corner to exchange gifts. The new computers are used heavily for homework and personal projects. Teens frequently use the corner and the computers in pairs and in groups; one goal of the project was to provide a space where teens could work collaboratively. Tutoring is also a popular use of the corner.

Numbers of Young Adults Reached

The numbers of teens reached is difficult to quantify, as many teens use the space without triggering any of the library's statistical measures. As of May 30, 2007, however, 323 teens had registered for library cards countywide since the kickoff on February 24, 2007—a 63 percent increase over the same period last year. At the Asheboro headquarters library, where the Teen Corner project was centered, 139 teens had obtained library cards since the project began—a 121 percent increase over the same period last year. Another 433 teens countywide have traded their old library cards for the new teen cards since the kickoff.

Numbers of Staff and Volunteers

Eight staff members have been primarily involved in the project. All staff participated in a workshop on services to teens presented by a former youth services consultant for the State Library of North Carolina. Volunteers have included an interior designer who contributed her professional services, five members of the Friends of the Library or Asheboro Library Foundation, and the five members of the Teen Advisory Board.

Funding and Budget Figures

The Asheboro Library Foundation provided $16,500 for the purchase of eight upholstered tablet arm chairs from Jack Cartwright Inc. in High Point, North Carolina, and upholstery fabric from Maharam; eight Caper task chairs for four new computer stations; temporary computer desks; and a permanent, skateboard-shaped computer table to be custom made at a later date.

The LSTA marketing grant provided $15,611 matched by $1,562 from the library budget for logo design and other graphics; the teen library card; four issues of the teen newsletter; poster and sign holders; ALA Read and other posters; banners; material for welcome kits for new teen card recipients including logo-branded bags, brochures, and bookmarks; other printed marketing material; and a computer and wide-carriage printer for continuing graphic work.

The Friends of the Library provided $1,791 for painting, wallpaper, decal work, commissioned art, and kickoff day entertainment (a rock band made up of local teens and a Mexican folk dance group).

The Jared Haft Goldstein Foundation, which supports the library's collection of health resources, provided $949.61 for the purchase of a teen health reference set.

From its operating budget, the library provided $5,231.80 for four computers, two printers, and software including Office Professional, Roxio Easy Media Creator, and Deep Freeze for each computer. Staff hours were considered part of normal library operations and were not budgeted per se.

Marketing

Marketing was and is an integral part of the project. In addition to the material furnished by the LSTA grant, the library has heavily promoted the Teen Corner and related events in its monthly newsletter distributed to 1,000 Friends, elected officials, and other community members; on its Web site and blogs; in local newspapers via news releases; and through contacts with school media coordinators. The Teen Corner newsletter is distributed primarily through fifteen middle and high school media centers. Viral marketing also has had an impact; the library staff continue to hear reports of teens showing off their new library cards to their friends at school, and the library staff have seen the same thing happen in the library. All newly registered teens are issued the teen-branded card; those who already have cards can trade in their old card for the new one at no charge.

Youth Participation

In spring 2006, a library science student surveyed teen users of the library and of school media centers in the community. Library staff used these results, which particularly pointed up the need for a place specifically for teens in the library, in writing the LSTA grant proposal and planning the Teen Corner project. In October 2006, the TAB was formed and teens were solicited to volunteer. With five continuously participating teens and several occasional attendees, the TAB meets monthly. The TAB has had key input on all subsequent parts of the project, including monthly teen programs. The group helped plan the Teen Corner kickoff and played host during the day—and at a prior reception for donors, cutting the ribbon to the area in preference to dignitaries in attendance such as the mayor and county manager.

Evaluation

The program is still new, but evaluation measures will center on the following: the increase in the number of teen library cardholders, the increase in circulation of library materials to teens, and the number of teens trading old library cards for the new teen cards. Preliminary numbers look great. Statistics show a 79 percent increase in the number of library cards issued to teens in March 2007 (127 cards countywide) versus the monthly average for 2006 (71 per month), and a 26 percent increase in the circulation of library material to teens in comparison to the 2006 monthly average. This program greatly improved the image of the library in teens' eyes by identifying them as a unique part of service population with unique needs (as evidenced by the popularity of teen-branded library card). It also serves as an inspiration for innovation in other aspects of library service.

Possible improvements to the program could include: better organization, a better timeline, the inclusion of more lead time for graphics and printing, and clearly delineated staff roles and duties.

Suggested Variations

Instead of a complete teen-designed card, teen welcome bags could be given to teens who signed up for a library card. It would provide information about the library, teen services, and how to get involved in programming and the TAB.

A teen area with routinely changing displays in teen areas would draw attention. Libraries could find innovative ways to display materials for teens.

Staff could use welcome kits and other promotional material outside the library, such as school career fairs, mall events, and more.

Relevance to
Overall Young Adult Services

The Teen Corner project has provided a shot in the arm to the library's previously passive efforts to serve teens. In essence, it did not fit into existing services as much as it continues to reorient existing services and create a blueprint for the future. In response, several library branches are looking at ways to create or refurbish their own teen areas, and two have planned significant teen programming of their own during the summer reading programs. It has become clear that teens want to be the recipients of library services created especially for their age group and designed for their particular needs.

Resources

Tuccillo, Diane. *Library Teen Advisory Groups: A VOYA Guide*. Methuen, N.J.: Scarecrow Press, 2005.

two

Creative Teen Clubs

The description for this category covered regularly meeting teen groups based on a teen interest or groups that enhance library or literary experiences for teens. Even from the previously listed programs in the Enhancing Teen Spaces category, it is clear that the teen club can have a variety of themes or purposes. If a teen advisory group does not work at one school or public library, perhaps a club can follow an interest or a theme, such as a writing group or an anime club. Some of the other programs in this volume were run by teen clubs, but the three listed in this chapter have very distinctive themes.

Top Five Program

TITLE OF THE PROGRAM/SERVICE

Skateboarding Discussion Group

Albany Public Library, New Scotland Branch, Albany, New York

Type of program/service:
Series/ongoing program/service

Targeted audiences:
Middle School, Junior High, Senior High, At Risk

Name of contact person:
Melissa Wasilewski
wasilewm@uhls.lib.ny.us

Other categories for this program:
Services Under $100

Program Summary

The Skateboarding Discussion Group is a weekly meeting of teens interested in skateboarding culture. Each week the group participates in one or more of the following activities:

- critiquing an interview or article about skateboarding;
- watching skateboarding videos on DVD or from the Internet;
- recommending materials to be purchased for the collection;
- developing content for use in a blog or zine, including maps, guides, photos, videos, fiction, art, advice columns, events announcements, and reviews of media or gear; or
- collaborating with other teen groups to communicate teen needs to design professionals during upcoming library facility renovations, including the design of teen spaces.

A library school student named Damon Volce, who was also a semi-pro skateboarder, moderated the first year of the skate program. Teens subsequently requested the group be self-moderated allowing teen volunteers and guest speakers to select and present content.

Steps

The program was a skateboarding program first called Roll into A Book, but in the end, no books were read. The goal was to attract the teens who skateboarded outside into the library.

Then Volce offered skateboard videos viewing and discussion. It is popular in skateboard culture to view skateboard videos and chat about them.

The next goal was to develop repeat customers from this group. A skate trivia contest was offered where the winner would get a prize at the next meeting. Even teens who worked at the library tried to win the contest!

Slap Skateboard magazine and the Shelter Skatepark were solicited to donate prizes. They gave the library T-shirts, magazine subscriptions, free skate passes, and tons of stickers and posters. Because the shelter was local, the skaters knew about it and loved to skate there.

The group enjoyed gossip about skateboarding after viewing videos, such as what riders had switched teams. Because the group was so active they would also enjoy watching YouTube to see their favorite riders or even watch the guys from the local shop.

Description of Library

Albany Public Library, in Albany, New York, is an urban public library system serving a community of 97,000 residents. New Scotland Branch is a small branch of Albany Public Library, housed in a 1,600-square-foot portion of an elementary school building for sixty-three years. The New Scotland Branch has one full-time and one part-time librarian and one full-time and one part-time clerk. New Scotland Branch is open forty-eight hours a week.

The space directly outside the library entrance is a popular location for skateboarding. Skateboarders had been a part of the landscape of the outdoors of the library for many years without any library programming developed to serve them. The location had never had programming for teens at all prior to the skateboarding program.

Intended Audience and Demographics

Teens who are active skateboarders or fans were the primary targeted audience for this program.

The New Scotland neighborhood is a truly diverse area. The largest English speaking contingents include African Americans, Orthodox Jews, and Caucasians. The area also has a large amount of first-generation English-speakers from the far reaches of the globe. The largest communities of these hail from the Philippines, China, the former Yugoslavia, and various African nations. There are six traditional high schools serving the area—one private secular, three private parochial, one military, and one public. There is also an alternative high school, a high school for teens with special needs, and a school for troubled girls. The library is within walking distance from many homes and institutions serving foster children.

Rationale

The skateboarding program was an important first step to legitimizing skateboarding to the community as a pastime as respectable and beneficial to the participants as other more mainstream sports. The community had at times marginalized and even verbally abused this group because of their activities outside the library. By accepting them into the larger community and making them stakeholders in the services offered by the library, the library staff gives skateboarders a forum in which they can thoughtfully discuss how they would like to interact with the community. Teen library behavior improved due to mutual acceptance between staff and teens and mutual accountability. Staff got to know reading levels, interests, and habits of a segment of a user group who also planned and used more library services.

Being welcomed into the library as a valuable patron rather than a nuisance, teen participants more readily explore what the library has to offer, get to know staff, and become accustomed to communicating information needs. The librarian is then seen as an enthusiastic advocate for skateboarders with library patrons and law enforcement. Teens then experience a sense of participation in and stewardship of the library. Literacy is increased through exposure to targeted high-interest materials for recreational use. Teens experience equity of access by being treated like a valued customer and being offered added services. Teens become aware that material related to pop culture and their specific interests are available onsite or from other libraries in systems.

Number of Young Adults Reached

The program was attended a total of two hundred times.

Number of Staff and Volunteers

One staff member facilitated the group by providing space, equipment, promotion, and guidance. One intern designed the format of the group, developed promotional materials, promoted, and led the group.

Funding and Budget Figures

The program was cosponsored by a local for-profit indoor skateboarding arena and skate shop, but this partnership only served to help with marketing and promotion. The program did not require any extra staff hours for planning or execution. Intern supervision and program development is already built in to the job description of the supervising staff member. No monies were spent on materials. All equipment used existed in-system previously, and a minimal amount of staff time was used to transport the equipment to the branch. Relevant costs included copy machine use, and occasional refreshments, totaling no more than $10 per session. These monies were drawn from the regular programming budget. Another library beginning this initiative could spend up to $30 for each skateboard video, but the library could then add them to their DVD collection.

Marketing

Promotional flyers were handed out. The librarian and intern personally invited individuals in and outside of the library. Other advertising was done in the library newsletter, local newspapers, the library Web site and branch calendar, the library MySpace page, and through word of mouth.

Youth Participation

Youth decided the dates and times of meetings, promoted the events to other youth, brought in content for discussion, requested a minimum age for participation, and evaluated the program resulting in teen-suggested changes in format and leadership to be implemented in the next incarnation.

Evaluation

Being the first teen program at the branch, the first teen program of its kind in the area, and the only program targeting teen boys during the summer, there was no data for comparison. But the program can be evaluated as a success in other ways. Teenage boys began coming to the library and using the resources. It made the kids feel good that the local library was supporting a pastime that is sometimes looked down upon in society. Other families liked to watch the videos and that could spark interest for future skateboarders. The kids all walked away with skate park passes and subscriptions to *Slap Skateboarding* magazine. The teens also learned how to navigate the Web better by working on the trivia contest.

Changes to the program could include more reading in the program. The main focus at first was to just get the kids in the door and watching the videos. The next step would have been to try and get them in the habit of picking up a book rather than just the computer or the TV.

Suggested Variations

Books or magazines could be added to the videos being discussed. There are a number of great books written by skateboarders for skateboarders. Also the use of skateboard magazines is always a plus. Libraries with a larger budget might help promote technology usage, by having someone come in and teach the group how to film and edit videos. Another speaker could be someone who makes skateboards and could give teens a view of how the board transformed from tree to final product. Being very open minded with this group of kids is the key to the success of the program. The librarian must show respect to the teen as well as skateboarding and its culture. Art and music are also very big in the skateboard world and both of those cultures can add some extra flavor to the program.

Relevance to Overall Young Adult Services

The skateboarding program has been an important first step to change the organizational culture that has asserted that teens will not attend library programming. It proves the efficacy of high-interest clubs to develop teens to take on high levels of stewardship and participate in library/teen partnerships. Evidence of teens becoming increasingly responsible due to opportunities for leadership created by library programs supports the design of more such opportunities, guiding the organization toward high-quality library service to young adults and a demonstrated commitment to youth development.

Flyer for the Albany Public Library skateboarding program

Energy: A Teen Leadership Academy

**Homer Public Library District,
Homer Glen, Illinois**

Type of program/service:
Series/ongoing program/service

Targeted audience:
Senior High

Name of contact person:
Alexandra Tyle Annen
atyle@homerlibrary.org

Program Summary

Energy is a teen leadership academy. The academy aims to help create youth leaders who will assume leadership roles throughout the community. The academy runs six months; the first four months begin with presentations, the last two months end with volunteer work. Teens are encouraged to attend the academy to gain skills that can be utilized throughout life while having fun doing so! Participation in this academy will look impressive on college applications and resumes.

Steps

A breakdown of specific steps for staff would include:

- contact speakers and arrange schedule;
- create logo, publicity material, and application;
- send out press releases;
- contact local businesses about donating food for events;
- evaluate applications and send out acceptance letters;
- send out e-mail reminders to speakers as their speaking engagement nears;
- send out e-mail reminders to participants about upcoming events;
- send out surveys after every few presentations for feedback;
- arrange volunteer hours;
- send out reminders to those participants who will fall short of volunteer requirements;
- create certificates; and
- distribute award certificates.

Description of Library

Homer Township Library serves one of the fastest-growing communities in Illinois. According to the 2003 Census Bureau estimate, the Homer Township Library services a population of 32,000 residents, 17,000 of which hold library cards. This community has experienced tremendous population growth over the last decade.

The purpose of the Homer Township Public Library District is to serve the informational, cultural, and educational needs of all Homer residents, regardless of age, sex, educational background, race, or creed.

Intended Audience and Demographics

Energy: A Teen Leadership Academy is designed to meet the needs of teenagers at local high schools. According to the latest U.S. Census figures, Homer Township's population has increased 34 percent between 1990 and 2000 (from 21,456 to 28,992). The people between the ages of 10 and 19 total over 4,783. The Northeastern Illinois Planning Commission projections forecast more than a 50 percent increase in population over the next twenty years.

Area teenagers attend Lockport Township High School. The Lockport Township High School demographics for 2006 are Caucasian, 55 percent; African American, 19.9 percent; Latino, 18.7 percent; Asian, 3.8 percent; Native American, .2 percent; and multiracial, 1.8 percent. Lockport Township High School is currently on academic watch status, which means that the school has failed to make the state's requirement of "adequate yearly progress" after four annual calculations of missing the adequate yearly progress requirement.

Rationale

Energy is designed to meet the needs of the underserved high school segment of the population. Within the last few years, the Homer Township Library has begun to increase teen programming. The librarians noticed that many of the teen participants were junior high students. The library was having difficulties attracting high school students to the teen programs. After discussing this situation with local teenagers, the library realized that many high school teenagers feel a large age gap between high school and junior high.

The library decided to create special library programs for high school students. The Homer Township Library decided to create a long-term teen leadership program, Energy, which would prepare teenagers with the skills needed to become productive and contributing members of the Homer Township community. Energy would help create youth leaders who would participate in leadership roles throughout the community. The library's goal was to challenge teenagers to enhance and promote themselves to the community. The program was designed to improve teenagers' self-worth, self-esteem, and confidence with their new skills and abilities. Participation in this program would be a great resume builder for jobs and college applications. After viewing the success of this program, the library has decided to make Energy an annual program.

Teenagers were required to apply for the Energy program because this was a long-term program. The library had thirty-three teenagers apply for the first year's program. During the first few months of the program, teen participants were required to attend the opening session and four presentations. Fifteen presenters focused on topics such as leadership, teambuilding, communication, ethical decision making, creative thinking, and sense of community. All of the individual programs, with the exception of the opening program, were open to all teenagers.

During the last two months, participants are required to volunteer at the library. They help with summer reading programs like summer reading desk, book buddies, and readers and leaders. If participants are unable to volunteer at the library, they may volunteer at another organization, subject to approval by library staff.

During the volunteer months (summer), the library podcast career interviews with young professionals. These interviews provided high schools students with information on different careers to better help them to choose careers or college majors.

Numbers of Young Adults Reached

There are thirty-three teenagers enrolled in Energy. All Energy programs, with the exception of the opening session, are open to the public. In addition to those enrolled in the Energy program, the library staff has had many other teenagers attend sessions. Opening the programs to all community teenagers helps promote the Energy program for future years. Monthly teen attendance to programs almost quadrupled.

Numbers of Staff and Volunteers

One staff member, the adult services director, designed and implemented the program. The administrative assistant contacted various community restaurants to donate food for the events. The opening sessions required four staff members to set up and supervise.

Funding and Budget Figures

These costs could vary; for example, libraries can seek volunteer speakers from local colleges, businesses, or local leaders.

Opening session: DJ	$100
Banquet hall and food	$200
Closing session: BMX Rider	$399

Many individuals spoke for free; others were hired for adult services programs and were therefore compensated with money earmarked from the adult services budget. Food was donated by various community organizations.

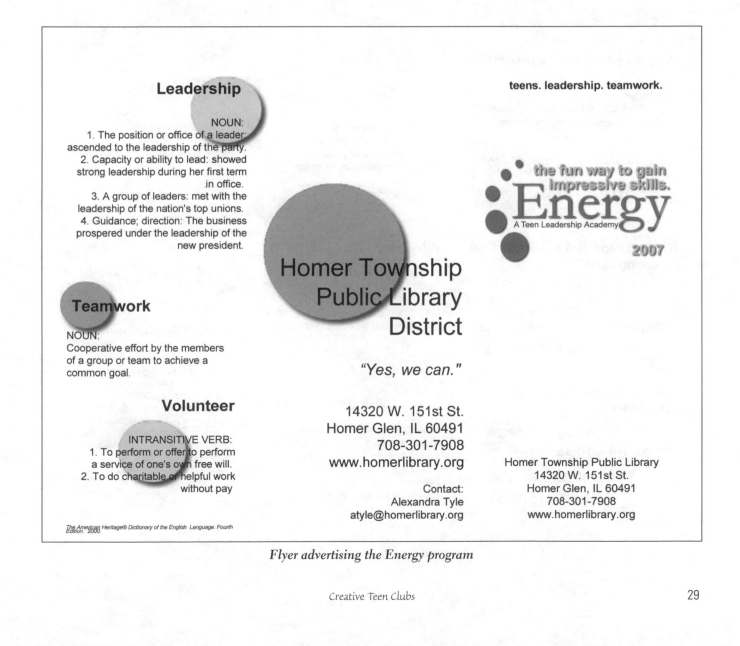

Flyer advertising the Energy program

Marketing

The library designed a logo for Energy to be used on all publicity materials, e-mails, and blog postings. A brochure was created to explain the leadership academy, along with an event schedule, application, and business card. Publicity began in November 2006.

The library created posters stating: "Energy—Look for more information in December 2006." When December arrived, new posters describing the program replaced the old posters. Posters were placed on various community boards. The library also sent out an e-mail to the library system discussion list inviting nearby libraries to help publicize the program.

Letters and brochures were sent to local public and private schools. Teachers were invited to help advertise the events. The library also sent out press releases to the local newspapers.

Youth Participation

The library was interested in obtaining teen input on the program. Existing young adult committee members, teen webbies (technology club), library pages, and teen patrons were consulted for suggestions and discussions during the planning and implementation of the program. Teens were asked to evaluate each individual presentation and the program as a whole. As the library

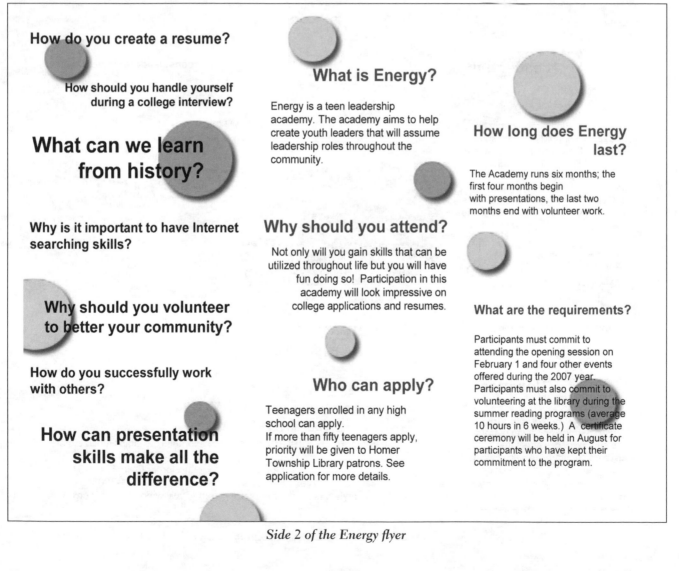

How do you create a resume?

How should you handle yourself during a college interview?

What can we learn from history?

Why is it important to have Internet searching skills?

Why should you volunteer to better your community?

How do you successfully work with others?

How can presentation skills make all the difference?

What is Energy?

Energy is a teen leadership academy. The academy aims to help create youth leaders that will assume leadership roles throughout the community.

Why should you attend?

Not only will you gain skills that can be utilized throughout life but you will have fun doing so! Participation in this academy will look impressive on college applications and resumes.

Who can apply?

Teenagers enrolled in any high school can apply.
If more than fifty teenagers apply, priority will be given to Homer Township Library patrons. See application for more details.

How long does Energy last?

The Academy runs six months; the first four months begin with presentations, the last two months end with volunteer work.

What are the requirements?

Participants must commit to attending the opening session on February 1 and four other events offered during the 2007 year. Participants must also commit to volunteering at the library during the summer reading programs (average 10 hours in 6 weeks.) A certificate ceremony will be held in August for participants who have kept their commitment to the program.

Side 2 of the Energy flyer

plans the second annual Energy program, the first year's participants will be available to help plan presentations and make suggestions.

Evaluation

The library kept track of attendance of both Energy participants and other teens to Energy programs. After comparing monthly attendance to previous months, it was found that teen attendance to programs had almost quadrupled. The library created online surveys to evaluate the various programs, topics, and interest. These surveys will help staff design next year's Energy program. The library also encouraged dialogue with teen participants to obtain feedback on how the program was received by the target audience. The program challenged teenagers to enhance and promote themselves to the community. It also improved self-worth, self-esteem, and confidence. Staff received many positive comments about this program from teenagers, parents, community leaders, and other adults.

In future programs, staff will send publicity material to potential speakers so that they will have a better understanding of the program. The library will also have a backup plan in case a presenter cancels at the last minute, such as leadership and teambuilding activities, with a container of the materials needed ready.

Relevance to Overall Young Adult Services

The purpose of the Homer Township Public Library District is to serve the informational, cultural, and educational needs of all Homer residents, regardless of age, sex, educational background, race, or creed. Recently, the in-house young adult committee was formed and has begun to create and implement teen programming that meets the library goals. The Energy program has supplied the teen participants with skills that can be applied today and also utilized throughout life. The library has seen the need to bring teen programming and services into the library and has created new, innovative programs and services to meet these needs.

The X-Room

Volusia County Public Library System, Deltona, Florida

Type of program/service:
Series/ongoing program/service

Targeted audiences:
Middle School, Junior High, Senior High

Name of contact person:
Jonathan Dolce

Program Summary

The X-Room is a free, daily, after-school program for teens in grades 6 through 12 that meets from 3:45 to 4:45 p.m., Monday through Thursday, in the library auditorium. With the library movie license, a movie from the DVD collection is shown on Mondays and Tuesdays. Popcorn is available for free on these days, provided by the library association, with a popcorn station run by teens. On Wednesdays, the library staff have crafts, computer games, PlayStation games (the system and the games were all donated), cable TV (donated by Brighthouse), and a movie all going on simultaneously. The various stations are self-policed. Thursdays see the same lineup, minus the crafts, but with the option of drama, improv games, or readers' theater. Space is provided for card games, homework, or just chatting. Recent experimentation with how the group responds to being read to has been performed with some success and will continue.

Description of Library

Deltona Regional Library is the busiest library in the Volusia County library system in terms of patrons coming in the door, and has the number two ranking in circulation statistics. It is in the unique position of being within walking distance of an elementary school, a middle school, a high school, and a community college. Additionally, local bus service is available for teens from the high school on the other side of town. The library itself is built upon a scrub habitat, Lyonia Preserve at Section 16, and is maintained by the Environmental Management branch of the Volusia County government.

Intended Audience and Demographics

The X-Room is specifically designed for young adults in grades 6 through 12. With Galaxy Middle School next door, Deltona High School down the way, and Pine Ridge High School students being dropped off by local bus service at the library doorstep, many teens use the library. Galaxy Middle School has 1,700 students, Deltona High has 2,815 and Pine Ridge has 2,354. Of the three schools, there is an average student population of the following ethnicities: Latino, 23.2 percent; Caucasian, 65.9 percent; African American, 9.6 percent; Asian, 1.1 percent; and Native American, .3 percent. While 50 percent of the student population qualifies for subsidized meal programs, this is in line with the state average.

Rationale

The X-Room provides many different things: a safe haven for latchkey children; a respite after a long day at school; positive interaction with adult staff members; a positive library experience; a chance to interact with students from other schools, walks of life, and age groups; and opportunities for teens to volunteer their time for children and young adult programming and activities.

Research has supported the fact that children who are left unsupervised after school face greater risks and receive fewer rewards. The X-Room is a quality after-school program that provides children with the safety they need and reduces their chances of taking risks outside adult supervision. The adult and peer interaction in the X-Room aids in the teens' emotional development and teaches them respect for people different from themselves as well as ways to resolve conflict with other teens. All these factors lead to constructive support for development. With these social skills, teens will have greater self-confidence. Through enriching, creative projects, in a welcoming and comfortable environment, teens can express their feelings and handle frustration as well as find ways to channel their actions and emotions in a positive way. Creative projects would include crafts such as altered books, decorations for the young adult section, decorations for various children's and young adult programming, key chains, notepads, jewelry, assorted bead crafts, and much more. Creative dramatics, such as improvisational theater and readers' theater, offer outlets for creativity and spontaneity, as well as honing public speaking skills and quick, on-your-feet thinking. It is through creative dramatics that teens can express a range of emotions, gain confidence in front of their peers, and feel more comfortable in their own skin.

Numbers of Young Adults Reached

The X-Room serves approximately twenty children daily or about eighty children weekly. The X-Room schedule mirrors the local schools', so as long as school is in session, so is the X-Room. Annual X-Room events, such as the Teen Mardi Gras Dance Party, see an attendance of 150 or more teens, while slightly smaller events, such as the Heave-Ho! Party, X-Mas Party, and the End of School Party, see numbers closer to 70 teens in attendance each.

Number of Staff and Volunteers

The X-Room is staffed by two library assistants, one of whom is an MLS student. The library has a roving sheriff's deputy every day after school who will drop in on the X-Room. On Mondays and Tuesdays, volunteers from the X-Room run the movie day popcorn stand. Special events require more help, and may require as many as ten volunteers from the Teen Advisory Group, volunteers borrowed from the youth and circulation departments, two student workers from the children's section, several rotating staff members, and two sheriff's deputies.

Funding and Budget Figures

The X-Room is funded largely by Volusia County government as well as the Deltona Regional Library Association. The library assistants who run the X-Room are paid by Volusia County government as the X-Room program is a part of their regular duties, costing the taxpayer approximately $88 per week of operation (two library assistants costing $11 per hour, four days a week). Food and drink are provided by the library association, and amount to about $10 a week. Special programs require more funding. The three annual parties cost approximately $70 each, but the Mardi Gras Dance Party requires closer to $270. The Mardi Gras Dance Party requires more giveaways and larger amounts of food and drink. Flyers, posters, and other printed matter are provided by Volusia

County government as a part of normal library operational costs. Craft supplies are shared by the children's and young Adult's sections, but very little additional crafts supplies are purchased specifically for the X-Room. Furthermore, a great deal of materials are simply donated by the public, volunteers, or staff members. There is no formal X-Room budget, however the library association has never refused to reimburse a staff member for items purchased for the X-Room. The few outside speakers or presenters that have come to the X-Room have been completely pro bono.

Marketing

Marketing and promotion of the X-Room and its events are largely done in-house. Deltona Regional Library prints library events flyers monthly for the public, called "Happenings" as well as posting the Happenings on the home page. Local newspapers also print this same information. Larger events see poster-sized advertisements throughout the library. All X-Room participants are given tickets to events, which are actually mini-advertisements and have no bearing on whether they can attend. The library staff relies heavily on word-of-mouth advertising by satisfied X-Room attendees, and they are always encouraged to bring friends. The Mardi Gras Dance Party and other annual events are very much recruitment campaigns to increase attendance in the X-Room, and it works.

Youth Participation

Teen participants help pick the movies that the library staff show on Mondays and Tuesdays. Additionally, teens create all the decorations for the Teen Mardi Gras Dance Party, a project that can take up to eight weeks. Teens tend to help with clean up of all programs, as well. After

various events, teens fill out surveys, designed to give us feedback about how the library staff did and what the teens would like to see in the future. Surveys are occasionally used before a major program to determine food, drink, and music selection.

Evaluation

The X-Room continues as it always has with the attendance figures and five years of conceptual continuity. The surveys from events as well as teen feedback determine the future of the program, which continues to adjust to the students' wants and needs.

Relevance to Overall Young Adult Services

The X-Room is an integral part of young adult services at Deltona Regional Library. It is a recruitment tool for the Teen Advisory Group, a way of reaching the teens that check out items and spend time in the young adult section. It is also a litmus test for seeing how the library is doing in terms of programming and collection development. There is no other venue in which staff can get such accurate and up-to-date, relevant feedback. Ideas come from the teens including movie suggestions, collection input especially on DVDs and periodicals, as well as ideas for programming and crafts.

The X-Room is also a way for the library to inform teens about the latest things that are coming up in the library, such as the impending library expansion and what the teens can expect from the expanded services. On a smaller scale, the library staff can keep the teens posted on the latest items added to the collection—getting them excited and checking items out.

three

Reading Raves

The description for this category includes unique reading promotion initiatives, in the areas of readers' advisory, book discussion groups, incorporation of youth participation in library reading programs, services to reluctant readers or special needs readers, and so on. This is the most classic area of library programs for teens, but the following programs each provide twists and unique angles to appeal to today's teens.

Top Five Program

TITLE OF THE PROGRAM/SERVICE

Second Chance Books

Austin Public Library, Austin, Texas

Type of program/service:
Series/ongoing program/service

Targeted audiences:
Middle School, Junior High, Senior High, At Risk

Name of contact people:
Devona Carpenter, devona.carpenter@ci.austin.tx.us
and Brazos Price, brazos.price@ci.austin.tx.us

Other categories for this program:
Community Connections

Program Summary

Incarcerated teens have two options: sit in their cells or sit in their cells and read. The Second Chance Books project is a successful collaboration between the Austin Public Library (APL) and the Gardner Betts Juvenile Justice Center (GBJJC). This project exists to serve at-risk middle to high school teens in a pre- and post-adjudication facility. APL youth service librarians are at the facility weekly, bringing new books to the library and providing booktalks and readers' advisory to ensure that for these reluctant readers, the first book that they willingly pick up will not be their last. The program also includes a summer reading program and author visits to the incarcerated teens. Interacting with these same teens just weeks after placing a desired book in their hands shows a marked positive change in their attitudes toward reading as well as their reading behavior. Many of these teens had not ever previously completed a book on their own.

Steps

Those individuals wishing to duplicate the Second Chance books project must first find an institution that is willing to partner with the library to bring better library service to their residents.

A next important step is to plan the level of involvement at the partnering institution. Librarians could do as much as take over the collection development, offer programs, readers' advisory, and host regular book clubs. At a minimum, librarians should do readers' advisory on a regular basis. This is the backbone of Second Chance Books.

Planning expansion of the project is a good next step. This could be done by creating a strategic plan with periodic goals. This step is also very important for deciding what sort of data to collect about the project as well as how often.

At this point individuals have to dive in! Keeping a regular schedule at the partnering institution builds trust with both the partner and the kids. It can be a little frightening at first but interact-ing with these kids over books is ultimately very rewarding for them, your institution, and you.

Description of Library

Founded in 1926 with the motto "life-long learning," APL is an urban branch-based library system with twenty branch libraries, a history center, and a central library that offers patrons information and materials in a variety of formats to enable them to continue their learning experiences. APL is an award-winning system. Projects housed at APL, like Second Chance Books, have won numerous awards including the Texas Library Association Project of the Year Award in 2006.

The annual budget of the library exceeds $20 million and provides for 331 full-time staff members throughout the system. The 1,705,805 items held by the system are accessed by 66 percent of Austin residents, a total of more than 450,000 registered cardholders. These patrons visited the library 3,264,727 times last year and checked out a total of 3,373,408 items. They also volunteered more than 100,000 hours of their time to the library.

Intended Audience and Demographics

Second Chance Books serves youth who are incarcerated in a pre- and post-adjudication facility in Austin, Texas. Residents in these facilities reflect statewide norms of the Texas Youth Commission. As of 2006, 89 percent were boys while 11 percent were girls. Ethnic breakdowns were: Latino, 44 percent; African American, 34 percent; and Caucasian, 22 percent.

Rationale

Second Chance Books gives residents a positive avenue to interact as peers and equals through the regular book clubs. It allows residents to recommend and promote books to other residents. Above all else, it promotes reading for fun and as an escape. Many of these young people had never read for pleasure before participating and interacting with librarians at these facilities. To quote a resident at one of these facilities:

> How the library has helped me is by me reading and not being able to stop. The first time I came here is when it became my first time to read a book. It's been a tragedy to me coming back to juvenile but the only thing that is good is that now I love reading more than ever.

Number of Young Adults Reached

Approximately 12,800 young adults have been reached since the implementation of Second Chance Books in 2003, with 3,200 served each year.

Number of Staff and Volunteers

Three primary staff form the core of the team with an additional three staff members providing supplementary coverage. At its inception, the program required approximately four to five hours of staff time weekly. As the program has grown, the number of staff contributing has also grown to about eight hours of staff time weekly.

Funding and Budget Figures

The Austin Public Library provides paid staff time to work on this project for a total of approximately $15,000 yearly. This is derived from three staff at $20 per hour and five hours per week. In fiscal year 2007, Second Chance Books was given a $2,000 book budget from APL. Previous to this, books were purchased using grant and award monies and donations from the Friends of the

Library. Second Chance staff selects the books from the Friends of the Library book warehouse. The Friends of the Library has donated approximately $7,500 annually in books which can be broken down into 750 books at $10 per book.

In the past, new books and speakers were purchased from grant and award monies. In its history, Second Chance has been the recipient of a Tocker Foundation Grant for $500, the Texas Library Association Project of the Year Award for $1,000 and a James Patterson Page Turners Award for $5,000.

To reproduce this program, a system must provide staff time and funding for books. At minimum an entity that seeks to emulate this project should plan to spend approximately $500 on books annually. It is likely that the partnering institution has a line in the budget for the library that could help to supplement book costs. Another way to buttress the collection is to work with a Friends of the Library group or the surrounding community to receive donated books.

Marketing

All marketing is internal to the facility and is done via word of mouth.

Youth Participation

Youth participate in the selecting of books for the book clubs in addition to helping with selection for the collection as a whole. During the weekly visits, youth are asked what they would like to see in the library and eagerly suggest books for inclusion.

Evaluation

The program is evaluated in terms of number of youth served directly. In 2003 there were 3 special programs with 137 students attending. In 2004 there were 7 special programs with 240 students attending. Also in 2004 the project served 308 students during booktalk sessions and had 1,971 books circulated. In 2005 there were 10 special programs with 397 students attending. Also in 2005 the project served 880 students during booktalk sessions and 10,027 books circulated. In 2006 numbers increased and more staff were appointed to work on the program. It is likely that the upward trend will continue.

The Second Chance Books team is very good at connecting young people with books that are of interest to them. The program excels at listening and responding to the requests of the residents.

Planning for growth is the one area that Second Chance has had to incorporate haphazardly. Were this program to start again, a coherent plan would be in place that would allow for appropriate data collection.

Suggested Variations

This type of project—creating what amounts to a satellite branch in a non-traditional library location (in this case, a detention center) could be replicated in other non-traditional places. Alternatives could include halfway houses, drug treatment facilities, group homes, and so on.

Relevance to Overall Young Adult Services

The project ideally fits the mission of young adult services at the Austin Public Library as it very clearly connects books with young people. Programs further inspire the teens. For example, here are two poems written by two teens who took a writing workshop with Spike Gillespie as part of a Second Chance Books program:

I cry

I cry at night thinking where I'd be, if it
    wasn't for you

I'd be dead in the streets; I know that you
    really care,

Because if it wasn't for you're approval I
    wouldn't be here,

Realize that I'd been putting up a front,
    knowing

That it's hurting you because it's not what
    you want,

This is my poem to say thank you

To ya'll, finally you've helped me break
    down this wall.

Dear Family

Hi this letter is just letting ya'll know

That ya'll are the one's who's love will
    always show

No matter how much I hurt ya'll and
    pushed away

Ya'll always forgave and loved me
    another day

Through challenges in my life,

Ya'll have been there cheering
    me on

And forever ya'll stay my siblings,
    dad and mom

In addition, Second Chance Books received this letter from a noted young adult author who visited Gardner-Betts Detention Center as part of the program.

I am the author of several young-adult novels published by Simon & Schuster and Knopf/Random House, and I am writing to you in support of your foundation's award consideration for Second Chance Books in Austin, Texas. I had the privilege to do an author visit at the Gardner-Betts Detention Center through the Second Chance program last spring while I was on a book tour, and I could not have been more impressed with the program and the personnel involved with it. This program provides a truly unique and invaluable service to incarcerated teens—providing them with hope and self-worth through reading in the midst of very difficult circumstances. The adults who administer the program, particularly Devona Carpenter, offer wonderful commitment, inspiration, and much-needed warmth to these teens, who seem to respond in kind by becoming committed and passionate readers.

I couldn't recommend this program highly enough. If I could provide you with any additional support for Second Chance Books, please do not hesitate to contact me. Thank you for your consideration.

Best regards,

Rachel Cohn
www.rachelcohn.com
Author of *Gingerbread*, *Shrimp*, *Cupcake* and others.

Classic Literature for Teenagers

The New York Public Library (NYPL), New York, New York

Type of program/service:
Series/ongoing program/service

Targeted audiences:
Junior High, Senior High, At Risk

Name of contact person:
Hillias Jack Martin, hjmartin@nypl.org

Other categories:
Promotion of Award Winning Young Adult Literature,
Community Connections, Living in a Diverse World, Special Events

Program Summary

To address the documented decline in the reading of literature among the youngest adults, the New York Public Library's Office of Young Adult Services developed Classic Literature for Teenagers, a pilot project for teens based in the West Harlem neighborhood, served by the George Bruce Branch Library. The project utilizes classic texts––novels, poetry, and plays—to help teens learn and understand the many themes, cultures, and historical events described and apply this learning to their own lives. The genres have included biographies, memoirs, history, sciences, and mythology. Workshops, special events, and author visits were tailored to be appealing, challenging, relevant, and timely to a generation becoming aware of the themes in classic literature.

In addition, a committee of young adult librarians developed a booklist for wide distribution in New York City. New, Old, and Retold includes award-winning young adult books and a listing of classic texts that inspired those books. In some instances this pilot project gave the library the opportunity to work with organizations, work-shop leaders, and authors the library staff had not worked with previously. This project was made possible with the support of the Louis Calder Foundation.

Description of Library

Since its founding, the New York Public Library has provided free and open access to books and materials to encourage a love of reading, while offering a safe haven for young people. Today, the branch libraries' young adult holdings for users between 12 and 18 years of age are comprised of more than 350,000 print and non-print items.

Teenagers form an important and impressionable age group with varying maturity levels, interests, and reading ability. For these reasons, young adult collections are especially diverse with fiction that includes poetry, historical fiction, humor, fantasy, science fiction, and classics. Nonfiction titles support the school curriculum, describe career and educational opportunities and capitalize on teens' interests in learning independently about science, health, culture, and other topics.

Intended Audience and Demographics

The George Bruce Branch Library, located in Manhattan, serves a primarily African American (30 percent) and a Latino population (62 percent). The nearly 3,000 young adults ages 12 to 17 are evenly split between males and females; 43 percent live below the poverty level and nearly 60 percent speak a language other than English at home. The New York Public Library has branch libraries in three of New York City's five boroughs: Bronx, Manhattan, and Staten Island.

Rationale

Classic Literature for Teenagers events serve teens during the school day and during the after-school hours. The project also served teens as part of the library's annual, systemwide summer reading program. This special grant provided the opportunity to place a full-time senior young adult librarian on staff to reach out directly to school, community-based organizations, and to teens visiting the library during the out-of-school hours.

Numbers of Young Adults Reached

ASTRO Readers' Theater with Shellen Lubin
        Total attendance: 279

American Globe Theater/Shakespeare/ Stage Combat
        Total attendance: 116

American Place Theatre, *Literature to Life*
  Manchild in the Promised Land
  The Kite Runner
  Growing Up a Slave
  The Secret Life of Bees
  The Glass Castle
  Extremely Loud and Incredibly Close
  The House on Mango Street
        Total attendance: 269

Calligraphy with Elinor Holland
        Total attendance: 15

Heroes, Villians, Gods and Monsters: Classic Comics with Alex Simmons
        Total attendance: 11

Poetry Writing with Sydney A. Francis
        Total attendance: 12

Meet the Authors
  Frank Beddor   David Levithan
  Sharon Draper   E. Lockhart
  John Green   Rick Riordan
        Total attendance: 308

Number of Staff and Volunteers

From 2001 to mid-2005 the George Bruce Branch did not have a full-time young adult librarian, which made it difficult for the library's staff to adequately and effectively serve the teenage population in the neighborhood. Combined with an enthusiastic and compelling young adult librarian and ongoing outreach to local educational partners, the classics offerings at the library have demonstrated the library's ability to link to the curriculum offering a variety of diverse and challenging voices. The ongoing goal is to connect teenagers with the printed word, introduce them to the library, to develop a lifelong pleasure of reading, and to expand their horizons to include world voices speaking through the classics.

Funding and Budget Figures

Funding was provided by The Louis Calder Foundation from July 2005–June 2007.

Total Personnel	$115,950
Other than Personnel	$32,100
Total Direct Costs	**$148,050**
General Library Administration @ 15%	$22,200
Total Grant	**$170,250**

Marketing

Recruitment for participation ranged from direct appeal to local middle, alternative, and high school librarians; faculty members; administrators; and parent coordinators. All upcoming events for teens at NYPL are featured in the print and online calendars. Local teens, including members of the branch Teen Advisory Group suggested programs and special events for teens in consultation with the young adult librarian.

Evaluation

Local schools and students have responded positively to the programs and special events. Their enthusiasm is reflected in continued high attendance and related reference inquiries. To keep young people interested and involved, the library has created diverse and varied programming that focuses on literary works of high merit in a variety of genres.

In particular, the readers' theater programs and theatrical presentations have proved to be a very engaging way to draw teens into readings and discussions of classic texts. The programming has been greatly enhanced by follow-up discussions facilitated by program presenters and the young adult librarian. The mix has included workshops introducing Shakespeare and stage combat as well as solo theatrical events from The American Place Theatre's *Literature to Life* program.

Meet the author events generate their own special kind of excitement! Visiting authors whose works have been inspired by the classics included Frank Beddor (*The Looking Glass Wars*); Sharon Draper (*Romiette and Julio*); David Levithan (*Marly's Ghost*); E. Lockhart (*Fly on the Wall*); and Rick Riordan (*The Lightning Thief*).

Additional arts programs have included opportunities to create poetry, classes on classic calligraphy, and a workshop to create comics based on heroes, villains, gods, and monsters. Local teens are currently creating a podcast inspired by their introduction to classic literature. Their voices are featured on NYPL's Web site for teens, TeenLink (http://teenlink.nypl.org). Click on "Turn It Up @ the Library, NYC Teens Talk Out Loud."

Relevance to Overall Young Adult Services

The success of the pilot at the George Bruce Branch Library has allowed NYPL to test a project model that can be adapted for other branch libraries throughout the New York Public Library. Since 2004, the library has undergone a massive staff training initiative called Everyone Serves Youth funded by the Wallace Foundation. The goal of the training is to help all staff provide quality service to children and teens, foster sensitivity among staff, and increase the comfort level of both staff and youth during interactions at the library. The end result is that younger library patrons are being better served, and the library is creating a foundation of service for a new generation of users. Pilot projects, such as Classic Literature for Teens, have provided unique opportunities to test innovative ideas and to pair dynamic librarians with creative institutional and educational partners.

ABC Café

Virginia School for the Deaf and the Blind, Blind Department, Staunton, Virginia

Type of program/service:
Series/ongoing program/service

Targeted audiences:
Middle School, Senior High, Special Needs
(blind/visually-impaired)

Name of contact person:
Margaret Robison, Librarian,
margaret.robison@vsdbs.virginia.gov

Other categories:
Reading Raves, Services under $100

Program Summary

Librarian Margaret Robison had a moment of inspiration while trying to figure out how to encourage more students to use the library at this public, state-operated school for deaf and blind students. She envisioned the library as a trendy, Greenwich Village-style atmosphere in which students could eat, drink, and listen to fantastic literature. She thought that a place with comfy chairs, tables, soft lighting, music, and drinks just might be the trick to entice students to enter the library. It worked! The students are the delighted guests of the trendy ABC Café (no tips required). Each session begins with staff greeting the students as if they are visiting a restaurant. Music is playing and the students chat while the staff take the orders for drinks. The audiobook is then started and the students listen to the story while they eat lunch and sip on a yummy latte (decaffeinated) or lemon iced tea (drink choices change weekly).

Steps

The Virginia School for the Deaf and the Blind (VSDB) maintains two schools on its campus: one for the deaf and one for the blind. Each school has a separate library. The Theresa Stojek Library in the blind department serves all the blind and visually impaired students, primarily with fiction in Braille, large print, and audio formats. The enrollment in this department consists primarily of blind and visually-impaired middle and high school aged students ages 11 to 21.

The campus also offers a third library, a satellite library, separate from the deaf and blind department libraries, which is open during after-school hours for the residential students. It is in this satellite library that the ABC Café is set up. The library is a long rectangular room. It features four sections: (1) shelves of books and paperback display units and a story area for younger students; (2) a bank of computers set up along the wall; (3)

the café area with pedestal tables and chairs; and (4) a serving area with sink, shelving, and a long counter.

The ABC Café is a club for blind and visually-impaired students who enjoy listening to recorded books. The purpose of the club is to promote the enjoyment of literature as a leisure activity and to develop critical listening skills. The club is sponsored by Margaret Robison, library media specialist, and Michelle Butcher, teacher/library assistant.

The club meets twice a week on Wednesdays and Thursdays in the satellite library during lunch. The lunch period is thirty-five minutes. Lunches for student participants are brought from the cafeteria to the library by the teacher/library assistant. A selection of beverages is also offered to students while they listen to the audiobook. During the lunch period, students listen, eat, and discuss. By having these meetings during lunch, all students have equal opportunities to participate, including day students and those involved in extra-curricular activities.

Each audiobook takes four to six weeks to complete. The members choose the book for each new listening session from a list of titles developed by the sponsors with recommendations and suggestions from the students. The audiobooks are not purchased, but borrowed from the local public libraries. If the book is a hit then staff make an effort to add to the library collection.

This is the format for the meetings. One of the sponsors brings lunches to the library and makes other preparations approximately fifteen minutes prior to the meeting. These preparations include heating water (or hot chocolate during the winter months), setting out the mugs and stirrers, setting out beverages (tea, coffee, hot chocolate, lemonade), setting the computer to an acoustic Internet radio station, and setting the audiobook to the correct place in the player.

Students enter and place an order for a beverage at the counter. The two sponsors serve as waitresses to prepare and deliver their orders. Each meeting has a flavor of the week—whether it be coffee, tea, hot chocolate, or lemonade. A poster on the library bulletin board highlights the flavors of the week plus they are announced over the PA system for the benefit of the blind students.

Acoustic background music is playing softly while students place their orders and are seated. Café tables and comfy lounge chairs are set up around the library for seating.

The audiobook plays for approximately twenty minutes while the students listen and eat their lunches. Listening is occasionally punctuated by discussions about the book.

At the conclusion of the lunch period, students return to class with one of the sponsors while the other sponsor cleans up, which involves cleaning off and wiping down tables, returning unused supplies to the cafeteria, disposing of the trash in the dumpster, and washing dishes.

To actually implement the ABC Café, the librarian wrote a proposal to administration that outlined the format and requirements in terms of time, facility, equipment, supplies, and money. Once approved, the library staff called a general introductory meeting open to all middle and high school blind/visually impaired students. During this meeting, students expressed support for the idea of an audiobook club. They voted on the name ABC Café and they also expressed an interest in redesigning a section of the Yates Library to make it a more comfortable environment conducive to listening and more appealing to middle and high school students. At this meeting students also gave us numerous suggested titles for audiobooks to consider and each identified their favorite literature genre—suspense, humor, adventure, fantasy, and so on. Among the guidelines for choosing audiobooks were:

- use only unabridged audiobooks;
- must have an excellent narrator and be a good quality recording; and
- either cassette or CD are acceptable.

Following the introductory meeting, the library staff developed a list of suggestions for supplies and equipment:

- Paint the walls or have a mural painted on one wall. (Staff suggested that the art department might take this on as a project.)
- Add one more couch (the library currently had one couch and four upholstered chairs).
- Add two to three more comfortable chairs.
- Purchase vinyl tablecloths for the four tables

Other necessary items included:

- a large area rug;
- cassette player;
- lamps for improved lighting;
- table decor;
- posters for the walls and bulletin boards;
- plants;
- a hot pot or other machine to heat water;
- mugs; and
- a selection of decaffeinated herbal and flavored tea, instant flavored decaffeinated coffee, hot chocolate, and flavored lemonade.

Although the proposal was approved, there was no money allotted. The supplies, equipment, and articles of decor that the library staff received were donated by staff and included: a large area rug, lamp, tablecloths, mugs, cassette player, microwave, coffee maker for heating water, tea towels, ice bucket, and a colorful throw for the couch. Sponsors spent some of their own money to purchase items for decor at the local dollar store. Condiments, napkins, utensils, as well as some flavors of hot chocolate were provided by the cafeteria. The other beverages were either donated or purchased by the sponsors.

Description of School

VSDB was established in 1839 by the General Assembly as a residential/day special education facility to serve hearing impaired and visually impaired children from birth through grade 12.

The school currently serves ninety-seven hearing impaired students, twenty-four visually impaired students and one deaf/blind student. Staff use audiovisual equipment and disability-tailored computer applications in the classrooms to provide students with the best education possible.

Most students reside on the campus. The school's residential program includes three dormitories for deaf students and one dormitory for blind students. Dormitories are staffed by houseparents who supervise students during after-school activities, homework and study hour, and off-campus events. As in regular public schools, all students have opportunities to participate in clubs, organizations, sports, and community events. Students are transported home every weekend. The club is targeted toward the visually impaired population.

Intended Audience and Demographics

This program is intended for the visually impaired students at VSDB, however, it could be accessible to students with sight, providing they are not deaf as this is an audio program. The student population within the blind department consists of twenty-four students from various communities, both rural and urban, across the state of Virginia.

Rationale

This program is very important to the visually impaired community at VSDB. Visually impaired students often cannot participate in many of the activities that their sighted peers can easily enjoy. Many clubs and sports are not accessible to this population of young people and although many groups will try to accommodate their needs, it in no way can equal the level of participation available to a sighted student. This club gives the students the opportunity to be part of a group that has a common goal and in which all can participate equally.

The adolescent population of visually impaired students is first and foremost a population of adolescents. Like all teenagers, they want to know what people are wearing, what music others are listening to, and what books they are reading. In short, they want to know what's popular with teenagers today. The ABC Café is one way they can read what other teens are reading and feel a part of teen culture.

Number of Young Adults Reached

Nine out of the twenty-four students participate on a regular basis. This is an average of 35 percent of the student population.

Number of Staff and Volunteers

The program is easily run by two staff members. The library staff enjoyed serving an average of nine to eleven students per book session. Being blind or visually impaired, students needed a little more supervision than most sighted students of the same age, but two staff members could handle the program with a larger group of students without disabilities. This gives a ratio of one staff to every four and a half students, which works well. Staff members feel that they could easily manage a total of fourteen students before needing assistance.

Other than the thirty-five minute lunch period during which the club meets two days a week, it took the sponsors approximately an hour of additional time each of those days to set up and clean up. Time was also required to search out audiobook titles and preview them for sound quality for approximately two hours prior to each new listening session. The total time spent per month is approximately fifteen hours.

Funding and Budget Figures

The food, napkins, and utensils come from the cafeteria. Furniture and accessories were reorganized to accommodate the new space requirements.

Specialty drinks, mugs, carpet, and all other goods were provided solely by donations. As mentioned, much of the equipment, supplies, and decor were donated by staff. There was no budget to work with. The audiobooks were borrowed from the local public library via a shared services agreement between the school and the public library. The library setup was conducive to a café format because it had a nice counter with laminate top and a sink with an outlet nearby and cabinets. Lunches and some other supplies were provided by the school at no cost.

A budget of approximately $500 would be very helpful to purchase equipment and supplies if donations are not allowed. A budget of that size should be adequate to purchase a cassette or CD player, water heater, microwave, decor items, and perhaps a mini-fridge.

Marketing

Marketing was very easy. Staff put up posters, sent e-mails, made announcements on the PA system, and visited the residential facility to recruit potential customers to the café.

Youth Participation

Students assisted with deciding on the format of the café, designing the café, and choosing a name. The students choose from a selection of three titles of books by voting. Students provide constant feedback for potential book titles and improvements to the café.

Evaluation

Evaluation is measured by student participation. The program began with eleven students and two declined after the first session to make a total of nine regular participants. Participation is consistent with students only missing due to extenuating circumstances (for example, lunch, detention, illness, and so on). The students provide positive, supportive, anecdotal comments and have expressed the desire to see the club continue next school year.

Here's what the students have to say about the ABC Café:

"It's AWESOME! I love it that I don't have to go to the cafeteria and the book is so funny!" —Brittany

"I wouldn't miss it for anything! It's the best part of my day"—Charlotte

"It's awesome because you get to listen to a good book while you eat good food. It doesn't get better than that!"—Kierra

"It's better to be someplace listening to a good book than in the cafeteria listening to screaming kids"—Monica

The excitement and enthusiasm of the students was inspiring for staff. They enjoyed the whole experience, from being able to eat somewhere other than the cafeteria, drinking cool beverages, listening to audiobooks, discussing books, and being served by staff. It helped to create a bond between staff with the students. Another plus was that the students who participated in the ABC Café began to frequent the library more often, not only to check out books, but also to seek suggestions for reading material.

The group realized after the first few sessions that twenty to twenty-five minutes during lunch was not adequate listening time. Even though the students enjoyed eating away from the cafeteria, they felt that the continuity of the story was disrupted by such short segments. Staff also felt that there was not enough time for good in-depth discussion about the book. The next year the ABC Café will be expanded as an extracurricular activity meeting for an hour a week, which will provide greater story continuity and lend itself to better discussion opportunities. Staff will continue to offer special beverages,and hope to provide snacks as well.

Staff pulled the café together in a very brief time—about one month. Although students had input about the format and setup of the café, they did not actually get the hands-on experience of physically helping set it up. If students were allowed to help with decor and arrangement it may increase their investment in the club.

A budget would be very helpful especially in purchasing equipment for the club such as a cassette or CD player; microwave; mini-fridge; and items for decor including carpeting, posters, paint, and so on.

Previewing the audiobooks would help to avoid technical problems. The program encountered problems a couple of times with a broken cassette tape and also with a CD that skipped.

Suggested Variations

The ABC Café would be well suited as a public library club or activity. A public library could appeal to a wider population of students. The public library could set up audiobook clubs aimed at specific age groups (older elementary, middle school, or high school).

Relevance to Overall Young Adult Services

The ABC Café promotes an appreciation of literature and encourages continuing interest in reading and listening to literature independently. Using audiobooks enhances students' listening skills and comprehension of auditory information. The ABC Café is compatible with the Virginia Standards of Learning, including, but not limited to, the following areas:

Gr. 6.2: The student will listen critically and express opinions in oral presentations.

Gr. 6.4: The student will read and demonstrate comprehension of a variety of fiction, narrative nonfiction, and poetry.

Gr. 7.1: The student will give and seek information in conversations, in group discussions, and in oral presentations.

Gr. 7.5: The student will read and demonstrate comprehension of a variety of fiction, narrative nonfiction, and poetry.

Gr. 8.5: The student will read and analyze a variety of narrative and poetic forms.

Resources

Recorded Books Catalog for audiobook summaries: www.recordedbooks.com

LM_NET archives were very helpful in researching library cafes and book cafes: www.eduref.org/lm_net/archive

YALSA's Amazing Audiobooks for Young Adults and Odyssey Award: www.ala.org/yalsa/booklists

Audiobook Review Sources

AudioFile magazine (www.audiofilemagazine.com) has audiobook reviews (current and archived) that include valuable information as to audio and narrator quality. It also contains profiles on many narrators.

Earphones Award by AudioFile: www.booksontape.com/awards.cfm/earphoneaw

Audio Publishers Association, Audie Award: www.audiopub.org

four

Community Connections

The description for this category invited applicants with excellent initiatives in programs or services that involve a close partnership with schools, public libraries, or agencies in the community. The work of today's young adult librarians moves far beyond the reach of the walls of the school or library building to find teens where they are and meet their needs. These sterling examples of community connections show the impact teen services can have outside of the library.

TITLE OF THE PROGRAM/SERVICE

Vera Casey Parenting Class

Berkeley Public Library, Berkeley, California

Type of program/service:
Series/ongoing program/service

Targeted audiences:
Middle School, Senior High, Intergenerational,
At Risk, Special Needs

Name of contact person:
Viola Dyas, vdyas@ci.berkeley.ca.us

Other categories:
Promotion of Award Winning Young Adult Literature,
Reading Raves, Living in a Diverse World

Program Summary

Professional public library staff provides facilitation of parenting classes for pregnant and parenting teens enrolled in the Vera Casey Program. This program is a collaborative comprising Berkeley Unified School District, the Public Health Department and YMCA/Head Start. The librarian-facilitated meetings include book discussions and scrapbooking projects. Library staff collaborates with Vera Casey staff in planning curriculum and sessions that address the life issues teen participants face as well as a venue for discussing these issues.

Teens earn high school credit for participating in this program. During the summers of 2006 and 2007, teen participants chose to meet at the public library to continue their book discussions. They received summer school credit for the summer sessions.

The public library also serves as a resource to Vera Casey staff in locating literacy services for program participants no longer able to be enrolled in the school district due to age or personal circumstances.

Description of Library

Berkeley Public Library, a medium-sized urban institution supported by an independent tax and governed by an independent trustee board, provides services to high school-aged community members through collections and programs at each of its five facilities. Four professional librarians are dedicated full time to these services, which include outreach to school, city, and neighborhood agencies. Library staff have worked with the public school district on a variety of collaboratively planned programs and ongoing services throughout the past fifteen years. Teen services staff include librarians with backgrounds in public health, English language instruction, and other endeavors closely allied with building and maintaining teen interest in literacy, information gathering, and evaluation. Staff reflect the com-

munity demographically. In addition to supporting a Teen Advisory Group, the library also hires high school students annually to assist with both clerical tasks and outreach efforts in the youth community.

Intended Audience and Demographics

The Vera Casey Program is open to all pregnant and parenting youth under 18—with most participants being 16- or 17-years old—in the Berkeley Unified School District. Teen mothers and fathers are referred to this entirely voluntary program to support the continuation of their education and to link them to public health services. Enrollment in school is not required for participation, but teen parents are encouraged to remain or re-enroll in school and receive academic case management to increase their chances of school success. Participants can now earn academic credit by participating in the Vera Casey Program Parenting Class, offered with support from Berkeley Public Library teen services staff.

The participants comprise a diverse ethnic mix, including Latina/Latino, African American, and multiracial youth. Program participants can remain active in Vera Casey until one year after high school graduation.

Berkeley's adolescent population comprises about 4 percent of the city's total population of 102,000. Berkeley's teens are ethnically and socioeconomically diverse. African American and Caucasian teens each account for about one third of the adolescent population, with the remaining third is comprised of Asian/Pacific Islander, Latino, American Indian, and multiracial youth. The 7 percent of teens who are English-language learners come from a wide variety of linguistic and ethnic backgrounds. Nearly 27 percent of all Berkeley teens qualify for free or reduced price lunches. Family configurations include two-parent households, households headed by single parents or grandparents, and looser constructs including independent living and residence in homeless shelters. About 2 percent of Berkeley's adolescents attend an alternative (continuation) public high school and about 4 percent of the city's teens attend private schools.

Rationale

The teens eligible for enrollment in the Vera Casey Parenting Class rarely have any previous experience with academic engagement, reflective discussion of literature, or access to the information needed to support their choices and circumstances. Public library participation in the program includes providing access to free books, discussions of stories involving characters and circumstances that are similar to those of the teens, and discussions that provide insight into their own lives and decisions. The scrapbooking projects provide the opportunity to build written records for their babies and consistent relationships with caring adults in the community. Library staff also make referrals to such services as the library's adult literacy program to improve the social welfare of Vera Casey participants no longer enrolled in high school.

Numbers of Young Adults Reached

About thirty teens are formally enrolled in the program at any one time; between nine and twelve are active and regular participants in the Parenting Class programming.

Number of Staff and Volunteer Hours

The Vera Casey Program is staffed by public health professionals who provide case management and links to services supporting healthy pregnancies and babies, academic success, and strong parenting skills. Public health staff for the Parenting Class include 10 percent of the time of a half-time case manager. This half-time posi-

tion is supported by the California Department of Education's average daily attendance allowance; $3,500 of the case manager's salary directly supports the Parenting Class. The public library component utilizes the work of one teen services librarian, with biannual planning sessions that also include a member of library management. Library staff commit eighty-five hours of planning and programming time to Vera Casey annually, at the cost of $2,900 in salaries.

Funding and Budget Figures

Public health staff obtain funding for food offered during Parenting Class meetings from the Berkeley Public Education Foundation. During the summer sessions, library staff provide food through the generosity of the Friends of the Library. Approximately $1,000 is spent on food for participants annually. Scrapbooking materials, at an annual cost of $400, are also purchased through funds from both the Berkeley Public Education Foundation (50 percent) and the Friends of the Library (50 percent). The library portion of program funding also includes give-away copies of discussion books. While this expense is usually funded by the Friends of the Library through its annual grant to teen services, the receipt of the Great Stories Club Award from ALA's Public Programs Office and YALSA in 2006 further augmented available resources for discussion books. In 2006, the Friends spent $170 on books for Vera Casey; in 2007, the Teen Services Friends grant for books to discuss and give away through the Vera Casey Program totaled $400.

Marketing

Because the Parenting Class addresses a group that is already enrolled in the Vera Casey Program, all marketing is internal to members of that program. Recruitment for the library's programming for Vera Casey participants is done by Vera

Casey staff and teens already participating in the Parenting Class.

Youth Participation

Participants in the program choose the books that are then featured in biweekly readings and discussions. Low reading skills prohibit many participants from reading the selected books independently. However, they demonstrate independence and positive regard for the program by getting themselves to each meeting. They actively listen to the librarian and peers (with sufficient reading comfort) who read aloud, and then take part in the ensuing discussions. They share pictures and stories of their babies with each other and with program staff.

Evaluation

Evaluation has been informal, through feedback toward planning subsequent sessions. Because there is no requirement that participants attend, the fact that they follow through by returning to subsequent sessions indicates positive evaluation. The teens requested that the program continue through the summer and school years at the library.

Typically, teens enter the program without library cards, but once inside the library, they register and begin to use borrowing privileges; this indicates that the target audience has indeed been underserved before entering the program and that they respond to the program goals of youth development, adolescent literacy, information literacy, learning and achievement, and equity of access in a positive and active way.

Meetings of the Parenting Class take place both in the community and at the library. Meetings at the library include trips to the children's library to discuss and select books for participants'

babies. Meetings, whether at the library or at the Vera Casey Center, are two hours in length and include focused reading and book discussion or scrapbooking, along with time for food and the exchange of information about progressing pregnancies and infant development.

In addition to reading and discussing the Great Stories Club choices of *First Part Last* by Angela Johnson and *Born Blue* by Han Nolan, the teens selected and found much to discuss in *Dancing Naked* by Shelly Hrdlitschka. They have selected the memoir *A Piece of Cake* by Cupcake Brown, for later sessions. The scrapbooking component is expanding into cross-generational literacy as program participants will be learning to create board books for their babies.

Relevance to Overall Young Adult Services

Teen services at Berkeley Public Library strives to be both inclusive and collaborative, outreach-centered rather than passive. Programs supported and currently undertaken by teen service staff include an urban book discussion group, outreach to the Black Infant Health Project operated by the city's public health department, the Earphone English collaboration with the school district's English language learners program, and a Teen Advisory Group engaged in a grant proposal for funding to redesign the Central Library's teen area.

The Vera Casey Parenting Class exemplifies many of the strengths teen services demonstrates through any of these other projects, including staff who look toward teens for program planning and implementation leadership, an institutional premium placed on community youth development, and advocacy on the parts of both individuals and the institution as a whole for youth and their healthy development.

Top Five Program

Teen Empowerment: A Motivational Summit (T.E.A.M.S.)

Cleveland Public Library, Cleveland, Ohio

Type of program/service:
Single program/special event

Targeted audiences:
Junior High, Senior High, At Risk

Name of contact person:
Rollie Welch, rwelch@cpl.org

Other categories:
Living in a Diverse World

Program Summary

Cleveland Public Library's first annual teen summit—Teen Empowerment: A Motivational Summit (T.E.A.M.S.)—took place over two days on March 30 and 31, 2007. The goal of the summit was to offer a forum enabling Cleveland teens to become engaged with organizations in the city that offer services to them. Events on March 30, were of a kickoff nature, featuring a motivational speaker and a demonstration of a local school's drum corps. The following day, fourteen breakout sessions provided a mix of information, speakers that motivated teens, and sessions that were exciting to teens. Examples of topics presented at the sessions were managing stress, resume building, being fit for life, organizing money, and the steps involved to enter college. More than twenty organizations provided information on passive display tables. And perhaps best of all, upon registering, teens received a free book.

Steps

Organized by the youth services department of Cleveland Public Library, the 2007 teen summit included the first event for a year-long initiative called Fit for Life, which is a grant awarded by the MetLife Foundation in conjunction with Libraries for the Future. Other organizations that participated in T.E.A.M.S. were Youth Opportunities Unlimited, YWCA, the Cleveland Cavaliers, and the Great Lakes Science Center.

Timing of when to hold the teen summit was a tricky decision due to the fact that in Ohio, especially in urban school districts, there is a strong emphasis on passing the Ohio Graduation Test (OGT). Schools discourage any form of distraction for the students. The dates of Friday, March 30, and Saturday, March 31, were chosen specifically with this concern in mind. The OGT ended on March 15 and the teen summit weekend was placed between the OGT final date and Cleveland Municipal School District's spring vacation.

Once the dates were selected, the teen summit was offered primarily to the teens living in the City of Cleveland. However, through the promotion of the event, and plain old-fashioned word of mouth, a number of teens from surrounding suburban communities attended the program.

Description of Library

Cleveland Public Library, consisting of the main library facility and twenty-eight branches, a mobile library unit, a bookmobile, and the Library for Blind and Physically Handicapped serves the City of Cleveland. Cleveland Public Library is also the home for the Ohio Center for the Book. Founded in 1869, Cleveland Public Library is considered one of the major urban library systems in the United States. Cleveland Public Library is also the leader of CLEVNET Library Consortium, which shares resources with thirty-one library systems in nine counties throughout Northeast Ohio.

Intended Audience and Demographics

The population of Cleveland is approximately 480,000 people with about 70,000 children and young adults included in that number. Cleveland is an economically depressed city with many at-risk, or disenfranchised, teens. The dropout rate for high schools is about 45 percent.

One of the early goals of the summit was to open doors for teens to discover where they could go to get help on social topics that they are confronted with daily. Older teens from grades 10 through 12 were the initial targeted age group, but the library staff soon learned parents and caregivers were very interested in this program and they voiced a need for middle school teens to be involved with the positive experience. The audience then included teens from grades 7 through 12, but the majority of teens who attended were ages 15 and 16.

Rationale

The teen services staff informally solicited the after-school crowds at several branches inquiring as to what would draw them to the summit. Popular responses were: how to get a job, music,

how to lose weight, and how to enter college. Sessions reflected their input. The sessions were: Chill Out (stress management), Drugs, Alcohol, Date Rape Awareness, Fit for Life (presented by two members of the Cleveland Cavaliers Dance Team), Game On (board game demonstrations), Making Music, DIVA (leadership for girls), Boys 2 Men (leadership for boys), Money Matters (managing your money), Urban Art and Music, Step Up to Higher Learning, Science and Technology, Put It in Writing (publishing your work), and Get Involved! (volunteerism).

The library facility served as a forum that enabled a significant number of organizations concerned with connecting with teens to come together in one weekend and at one location. The live interaction with representatives was a much more effective way to connect with teens than listing the organizations on the teen library Web page.

Number of Young Adults Reached

The two weeks before the summit saw a preregistration count of 410 teens. This early tabulation was important as the library ordered a box lunch for each teen. However, of the 410 registrants, only 179 of them picked up their session assignments on Saturday morning. The good news was that through the marketing of the radio station, approximately eighty-three teens were "walk-ups" and signed up on Saturday. Thus, the total number of attendance was 262 on a Saturday. The Friday kickoff event had about sixty-five teens and parents attending. Unused food was donated to the Cleveland Food Bank.

Number of Staff and Volunteers

Staff time was involved in the monthly meetings held each month for eight months prior to the program. Members of the young adult services staff met for three hours during the eight different meetings. The program was a two-day event, from 6 to 8:30 p.m. on Friday, March 30, 2007, and twenty-four staff members were involved on Saturday, March 31, 2007, from 8:30 a.m. to 5:00 p.m. The staff and security salaries were not incorporated into the budget.

Funding and Budget Figures

The concept of the summit was suggested about a year before the event and was funded as a budgeted item in the library's branches and outreach budget. Additional funding came from the Fit for Life grant awarded to Cleveland Public Library through MetLife Foundation of Hartford, Connecticut, in conjunction with Libraries for the Future. Funding budgeted by the library came to approximately $5,000 with matching funds of $5,000 coming from the Fit for Life grant. Over the course of eight months of planning, teen services staff members contacted representatives from local agencies and asked if they would be willing to participate. Many organizations became involved at no cost. They considered it important and an excellent opportunity to promote their services. However, several presenters did request compensation for their time. The highest honorarium was $300 and the lowest was $125. The total cost of presenters came to $850. However, more than 75 percent of the presenters did donate their time for free. One of the largest expenses was the box lunches provided for the teens, which came to approximately $1,800.

Marketing

The Fit for Life grant dollars were spent to promote the teen summit through a popular local radio station, Z107.9. They provided ten public service announcements during the week prior to the teen summit. They also provided a radio personality and celebrity musician—Mike Jones, a local rapper—who conducted an autograph session for the teen participants. This cooperation from the radio station helped spread the word about the summit much more effectively than the print flyer.

Evaluation

Success was determined by the simple fact that almost three hundred city teens (the maximum number of participants was four hundred due to facility limitations) gave up a full day on Saturday to attend a library-sponsored program. A written survey was distributed, but only 20 percent were filled out. Teens gave suggestions about condensing the day because the major complaint was the length of the day on Saturday. Some teens had to catch a bus at 8:00 a.m. and the summit ended at 3:30 p.m., which made for a long day for them. The opening remarks for the summit began at 10:00 a.m. Encouragingly, the teens asked for it to be done again and many commented on how important it was to hear positive things they can do in the community.

Two months after the summit, the library offices were still fielding requests from organizations to be part of next year's event and many teens are asking branch staff, "when are you gonna do that that again?"

The strengths of the program were to bring agencies that have a goal of connecting with Cleveland teens together in one location on one weekend. The teen summit was a blend of interesting, fun things to do combined with informative breakout sessions. A by-product of the event was that it was proven that a large number of inner-city teens could come together in a single setting and leave with a positive experience.

Nothing is for sure when planning a teen event! The first choice for a keynote speaker was Heisman Trophy winner, Troy Smith (a graduate of Cleveland schools) and he said he would love to, but his agent did not allow it. The second choice was Ted Ginn Sr., father of Ted Ginn Jr., the Ohio State football player. Ted Ginn Sr.

was the high school coach of Troy Smith and Ten Ginn Jr., plus nine other Ohio State players. Unfortunately, Mr. Ginn was hospitalized three days before the summit. The last minute fill-in speaker was a high school senior, Richard Starr, who discussed his rough past and gang involvement in the inner city and how he took it upon himself to be a leader in his school. Richard was very inspirational and will graduate with honors and plans to attend Ohio University.

The library staff has decided that the next summit will be on only one day. Fatigue set in for the teens (and staff) on Saturday afternoon. The library staff also wishes to set suggested goals that the library staff would want the presenters to cover rather than having them feel their way through the presentations.

Suggested Variations

The variations can be adapted to any community, or library that has agencies committed to dealing with teens. While Cleveland does have some larger organizations, the most effective presentations came from smaller agencies that were very enthusiastic about being part of the event.

Relevance to Overall Young Adult Services

T.E.A.M.S. fit directly into Cleveland Public Library's services to the community. As of May 6, 2003, the library listed five library service enhancements, one of them being more services to the children and young adults. Beyond that simple goal, the T.E.A.M.S. engaged teens in a community activity that brought a variety of services to them.

Hanging Out Rocks!

Loudoun County Public Library, Leesburg, Virginia

Type of program/service:
Series/ongoing program/service

Targeted audiences:
Middle School, Junior High, Senior High,
Intergenerational, At Risk

Name of contact person:
Linda Holtslander,
linda.holtslander@loudoun.gov

Program Summary

Loudoun County Public Library's Hanging Out Rocks! initiative successfully addressed the image of the library for teens. Through its services, programs, and volunteer opportunities the program created a welcoming environment where teens can be themselves, study, attend a program, listen to music, or just catch up with other teens. Specific to this commitment was the creation of a dedicated space for young people to meet in a safe and enriching environment on Friday evenings. Teens using the After Hours Teen Center at the library have access to activities dictated by the interest of the teens. The center now has eighty to one hundred young people taking part in the activities each week, with a total attendance of more than ten thousand since its inception.

While the focus of this component of service was the young adult, the library looked for ways that would blend the youth initiative into the other demographic groups it was serving in the community. Opportunities for programming with the Latino and immigrant residents were enhanced through job skill building for adults and teens. Older adults were served by teen volunteers who

assisted at senior centers, and opportunities for youth to participate as a reading buddies to preschool age children were developed.

Significant to the focus of the project was the goal-setting process for the year. The theme for the project would be Hanging Out Rocks!—a visual and verbal branding that intended to create a sense of belonging. Explicit areas of need had surfaced from the meetings with the teens, and the library moved forward to address these objectives with a wide continuum of county support. Supporters included: Loudoun County Public Schools; La Voz of Loudoun County; the Juvenile Detention Center; and the Loudoun County Department of Mental Health, Mental Retardation, and Substance Abuse. Fiscal support was received from the Loudoun Library Foundation, Inc., the Irwin Uran Gift Fund, MetLife Foundation, Washington Redskins Leadership Council, America Online, and special allocation through the County of Loudoun government.

While the focus was directed at the general community, a specific awareness was geared toward reaching the Loudoun County Board of Supervisors, engendering their continuous support and future fiscal allocations involving library teen activities, services, and a funding commitment to establish the After Hours Teen Center.

A critical factor was enhancing the image of the library as a place where teens could be themselves in a welcoming environment, study, attend a program, volunteer, listen to music, or just catch up with other teens. The established partners in the program were vital to the success. From distribution of posters and flyers, to bringing teens to events, they illustrated commitment and a buy-in to the mission of the project.

As a result of the specific focus and successful results that have emanated from the programs developed for teens by the Loudoun County Public Library, the library approached the Loudoun County Board of Supervisors for out-of-the-budget cycle funding to create a dedicated space for young people to meet on Friday evenings. Teens using the After Hours Teen Center have access to programs, gaming, music, food, and activities dictated by the interest of the teens. Beginning in June 2005, the Cascades Library, through a pilot program, became the place to be for teens on Friday evenings.

Description of Library

Located in one of the fastest-growing counties in the nation, the Loudoun County Public Library is situated thirty miles from Washington, D.C. Within the last ten years the county has changed from a largely undeveloped farming community to hundreds of planned neighborhoods that cover the county's 500 square mile area.

Loudoun County has added more than 150,000 people since 2000, increasing its population by 60 percent. Coupled with this growth has come the need to expand the library's collections, services, and programs to meet the growing cultural and age diversification of the community. The Latino population has increased 365 percent. The pre-school to early elementary group is the second-largest in the country. The school-age population has doubled since 1998, with thirty-seven new schools opening in the last decade. With a seven branch system, circulation of more

than 4 million and a 97 percent approval rating from the public, the Loudoun County Public Library reaches out to the community.

Intended Audience and Demographics

The Loudoun County Public Library has through its long-range planning process identified the areas that required a new and energized focus—among these was its services to teens. Concurrent to this examination of teen services was the initiation of the Loudoun County Board of Supervisors Youth Initiative. A plan was requested from the county departments to examine their services to teens and develop plans that would enhance their profile to this age group and develop a sense of place for youth. The library met this goal by creating a myriad of opportunities for teens in the library. From the After Hours Teen Center (winner of the 2006 American Library Association John Cotton Dana Award) to volunteer opportunities, to being a significant voice in the design of the 4,000 square foot self-enclosed teen area being designed for youth at the Rust Library, the system made teens a priority.

Rationale

In 2004, the Loudoun County Board of Supervisors undertook a major initiative focused on assessing current youth needs (grades 6 through 12) in the community. This led to the development of an action plan designed to engage the total community. Throughout the summer and fall of 2004, the Loudoun County Public Library, hosted one hundred Listening to Youth forums that brought teens together to answer two questions:

1. What did they see as constructive forces supporting growing up well in Loudoun County?
2. What did they see as the biggest challenges and major obstacles to growing up well in Loudoun County?

Participants recognized the strong sense of community in the county as well as identifying the lack of programs, resources, and dedicated teen space in the county. By naming their specific needs, the teens helped form the mission of the Loudoun County Public Library and its service to teens for 2005 and into the future.

Number of Young Adults Reached

Since 2005 more than 300 teen programs with an attendance of more than 2,000 have been offered at the library branches.

Number of Staff and Volunteers

Hanging Out Rocks! was developed under the Loudoun County Public Library's division of development and public relations. Linda Holtslander, division manager, and two public information specialists created and now oversee the program. Four staff and two security guards run the programs.

Funding and Budget Figures

The following is the current fiscal year 2008 budget established through the Loudoun County Board of Supervisors enhancement process to continue the weekly After Hours Teen Center.

Staffing/services

Permanent part-time salary and wages (four staff and two security guards)	$60,660
Programming	$11,500
Food supplies	$16,808
Educational and recreational	$10,000
TOTAL	$98,968

The Hanging Out Rocks! promotional budget reflects the funding necessary to reach the established goals of connecting to teens in the community through the establishment of the After Hours Teen Center. Corporate and foundation support provided the community connection necessary to the facilitation of the project.

Funding source

Loudoun Library Foundation, Inc. and the Irwin Uran Gift Fund	$15,000
Corporate support (AOL, Washington Redskins Leadership Council, MetLife Foundation)	$15,000
TOTAL	$30,000

Item	Quantity	Amount
Teen programming	100/year	$20,000
Printed materials (posters, flyers, bookmarks, brochures)	35,000	$5,000
Magnets	11,000	$1,000
T-shirts	1,000	$4,000
TOTAL		$30,000

Hanging Out Rocks! kept the continual focus on the library's mission to meet the stated goals of the teens, the principal goal being to give teens what they wanted—a "place of their own." On November 1, 2005, the Loudoun County Board of Supervisors voted and approved an allocation of $65,000 based on the success of the After Hours Teen Center, to continue to grant the teens of Loudoun County programs, resources, and a dedicated teen center in the county where Hanging Out Rocks! Subsequent to the initial budget, the After Hours Teen Center has received enhancements that now establish the fiscal year 2008 funding level at $98,968.

Marketing

The center was publicized in area schools with flyers and the distribution of 11,000 Teen Center magnets. Throughout the summer months, young people participated in the activities with the attendance growing each week. Continual marketing of the center's activities was done through the media and through the distribution of 50,000 copies of the summer reading program brochure, which promoted the After Hours Teen Center. The library displayed a large banner outside of the library that proclaimed the statement, "Hanging Out Rocks!" and the dates and time of the teen center's activities. The center now has more than one hundred young people taking part in the activities each week, with a total attendance of more than ten thousand since its inception.

Youth Participation

Acknowledging that the best source of information for what young adults need is young adults themselves, the library worked with teens in the community and members of the Loudoun County Public Library Teen Advisory Boards to set its 2005 project goals. Youth involvement was critical to the planning process, from informal one-on-one conversations to focus groups put together to define the role of the public library in their lives.

Evaluation

Hanging Out Rocks! surpassed the goals and objectives set by the library and was evaluated through the following:

Teen Involvement and Participation. The significant definer was to encourage the teens in the community to discover their library as a "place of their own." This was successfully demonstrated by the 50 percent increase in teen attendance at programs, and in particular at the After Hours Teen Center. Staff regularly evaluated the achievements of the center and its programming and adjusted the presentations to meet the comments from the teens. Perhaps the most telling observation by a youth participating in the teen center activities was: "We want to keep it going forever!"

Community Partnership. Hanging Out Rocks! provided a specific opportunity for the library system to develop a broad range of community partnerships. These ranged from refreshments provided by parents of teens to fiscal support from corporate donors. This project heightened the library's relationship with the Loudoun County Public Schools and involved many individuals who wished to find healthy, positive activities for young people. The program successfully reached teens with programming venues that encouraged reading, examined cultural differences, and provided role models for citizens with disabilities.

Teen Volunteer Opportunities. The unique volunteer opportunities for teens with the outreach services department heightened the continual focus the library had on breaking the stereotypes associated with its receptiveness to the interest of young people. Each day for ten weeks during the summer months, twelve to fourteen teens accompanied the outreach services team to an assistive living facility. Young people would read to the seniors, help them find books, and even play the piano. Teen participation in this program increased the number of volunteers by 30 percent and built a support system for future activities that would benefit from the assistance of young people. Additional programming that has allowed the teens to give back to their community included the 2007 Read-A-Thon, developed in partnership with the Loudoun Literacy Council. Teens in the community raised funds to support their reading at the library for six hours on a Saturday during National Library Week. The more than $4,000, which teens raised was given to the Loudoun Literacy Council, under the mission statement, "We will read so they can read!"

The project was well-planned and invited many agencies and individuals to participate. This factor allowed for better marketing. Paramount to this project was the need to adequately staff for the age group being served. Because the program is now the plan of service to teens, the

Marketing materials for Hanging Out Rocks!

library staff learns everyday from the youth in the community, and blends these suggestions into the future goals. The After Hours program profile is applicable to a variety of venues. The key to success is staff who will be able to work with the energy of the youth.

Relevance to Overall Young Adult Services

Never content to only serve a traditional segment of the population, the Loudoun County Public Library effectively works with the community system to develop and enhance its services. An ongoing partnership with the Loudoun County Public Schools includes author visits, electronic resources available from the library's Web page, and the presentation of the library's annual One Book, One Community. The selection for this program is made with a special emphasis on reaching youth and adults. Through a gift fund, copies of the book are given to every community member that selects to participate in the program. In 2006 the library selected *The Giver* by Lois Lowry as the One Book. More than 16,000 free copies of the book were distributed throughout the county and to the schools. In addition, 500 copies of the book in Spanish were given to the English as a Second Language high school classes.

Through a grant from the MetLife Foundation, the library developed a series of teen programs that were directed to reach the young people who participate in the homework club facilitated by the mental health, mental retardation, substance abuse division of the County government. The young people in this program face difficulties due to education, social, and economic factors. These teens participated in a series titled "Literacy through Art and Photography" and told the story of their life through multimedia presentations that included group writing, poetry, and photos.

Through a cooperative partnership with the Juvenile Detention Center the library has hosted a variety of grants. These include a National Endowment for the Humanities program titled "Poetic Justice," which brought poets into the facility to write poems about violence in society and the teens' own lives. The poetry written by the youth was scripted by a local high school and presented at a public program which featured Luis Rodriguez, poet, author, and community activist. All young adult authors who are brought to the community by Loudoun County Public Library are asked to speak to the detainees at the Juvenile Detention Center.

In 2006, forty teens met with the selected architects to "design" their library. When the Rust Library opens in 2008 there will be a 4,000 square foot enclosed Teen Library Center that will reflect the information literacy that is paramount to this age group. Subsequent buildings, including the 40,000 square foot Gum Spring Library (2009), will allocate space to young people, which will once again be designed with teen excitement and outlook.

Loudoun County Public Library has addressed one of the most significant issues in public librarianship today: how to create a library community for young adults. The answer to this problem was to develop a model that promotes the value of teens as library customers. The library has taken gigantic strides to bring the focus of its teen services, programs, and volunteer opportunities to the highest level of accomplishment. By bringing members of the community to the table to address this challenge, Loudoun County Public Library has created camaraderie of purpose, resources, and support, and has become an advocate for the unique needs of young adults. Hanging Out Rocks! is no longer a dream for Loudoun's teens; it has become a reality.

Resources

Loudoun County's One Book, One Community: www.lcpl.lib.va.us/onebook07/intro.htm

Teenie Boppers

Solano County Library, Fairfield Civic Center Branch, Fairfield, California

Type of program/service:
Series/ongoing program/service

Targeted audiences:
Senior High, At Risk, Teen Mothers

Name of contact person:
Sarah R. Krygier, sarahkry@yahoo.com

Summary

Fourteen to seventeen years-old, expecting or raising a child, and lacking transportation, the teens in the Young Mothers Program at Sem Yeto High School needed the library to come to them. Teenie Boppers met in the program's classroom for four, one-hour sessions. Each session consisted of an activity, a discussion, and a sharing of books (see chart for more details).

Description of Library

Solano County Library is a public library in the San Francisco Bay area (North Bay). Solano County Library offers professional, innovative, and cost-effective service by providing library materials, resources, information, entertainment, and lifelong learning opportunities to enrich the lives of the people of Solano County. Fairfield Civic Center Library is a downtown branch providing services to the more than 100,000 residents living in Fairfield, California. Customers within walking distance of the library live in lower class to lower middle-class neighborhoods.

Intended Audience and Demographics

The participants in Teenie Boppers are teenage girls who have chosen to attend Sem Yeto High

	Topic	Activity	Handouts	Books
2/1/2007	Goal setting	Goal worksheet, storytime, book survey	Folder with early literacy materials, guidelines for storytime, and so on.	Storybooks, YA fiction, YA ARCs (keep)
3/7/2007	College planning	Storytime, community college versus four year colleges, read aloud practice	Checklist for applying to college	Storybooks, YA fiction, parenting, college
4/4/2007	Career planning	Career quiz, discussion of possible careers	Career quiz "answers"	Storybooks, YA fiction, parenting, career
5/2/2007	Summary	Summary of what the library staff has learned, pick a free book	n/a	Free children's books, YA and children's titles for classroom

Summary of four Teenie Boppers sessions

School, an alternative high school in Fairfield, California. The girls have chosen to attend the program either because they have a child or are pregnant. The teens in the pilot round of the program ranged in age from fourteen to seventeen, from sophomores to seniors in high school. Two girls were in the second trimester of their pregnancies when the program began. All other participants already had babies or toddlers.

Approximately 12,046 of Fairfield residents fall in the 12 to 18 age range, with 51 percent female and 49 percent male. According to the Fairfield-Suisun Unified School District, 39.6 percent of students receive free or reduced lunches and 8 percent of the district's students in grades 7 through 12 are English learners. The students in the Young Mothers Program were of white, Latina, and African American descent. Latina students comprise approximately 31 percent of the population in the school, with African American students at 23 percent, and white at 29 percent.

Rationale

Teen moms need to know what the library staff can do for them, not just for their babies. Teens need regular attention from the library, and Teenie Boppers offers a monthly program. In addition to developing read-aloud skills, a portion of each session was devoted to the mothers becoming familiar with library resources for their own academic, professional, and personal benefit and a discussion on a teen-specific topic .

Teenie Boppers offers something that many of these teens would not otherwise receive—positive, dedicated attention. The mothers who participated in Teenie Boppers were able to see that the library and librarians do care and will make an effort to ensure that their needs are met. Other single parent and young parent programs in the Fairfield area provide for the mother and child's material needs but do not offer the kind of career and college assistance the library can. These mothers need to know that they can have a career

and to to college. Their options did not run out when they became pregnant.

Number of Young Adults Reached

Teenie Boppers reached twenty young adults. Ten to twelve teens attended each month.

Number of Staff and Volunteers

The young adult librarian met with two supervisors to discuss the initial proposal. The young adult librarian met with the principal of Sem Yeto High School and the two coordinators of the Young Mothers Program to outline the program's structure. Two teen volunteers assisted with preparing handouts and packets for the sessions. Primarily, one young adult librarian and two teen volunteers were needed to ensure the success of Teenie Boppers.

Funding and Budget Figures

No unique funding was required or sought for this pilot project. Approximately eighteen hours of the librarian's time was spent on this program––one and a half hours per session (including travel time), two hours preparation per session, four hours of initial meetings and later follow up. Funding for the librarian's time is provided by Solano County Library, and totaled $365.22 for eighteen hours of librarian time. The Friends of the Fairfield-Suisun Libraries provided $55 toward the purchase of new books at the close of the semester. The total for this program was then $420.22.

Marketing

With such a specific audience, Teenie Boppers required little marketing. The program developed after the young adult librarian contacted both the coordinators of the Young Mothers Program and the principal of Sem Yeto High School. Students at Sem Yeto High School do not have to attend each day, and the fact that certain teens made an effort to attend on session days speaks to the success of the program. In the days leading up to the sessions, the coordinators of Young Mothers Program reminded the teens that "Miss Sarah" would be coming that week. This encouraged the teens to return any books they had borrowed from the book bins and to attend school on the day of the program.

Youth Participation

Teenie Boppers does involve teens in the programming. The teens did not have the chance to ask for this program to begin, but they have asked that it continue. The teens also gave input on book topics or titles for inclusion in the book bins. The bins with children's materials are part of a library-developed product known as Big Blue Bins, plastic bins of books designed for check-out by teachers, day care providers and other professionals working with groups of children. At the first session, the young adult librarian distributed a book survey. The bins filled with young adult materials were specifically assembled for each session based on the results of the survey. Especially during the college and career planning sessions, the teens guided part of the discussion as they asked specific questions about college majors, childcare, and financial concerns. Future sessions will continue to be guided by the concerns and needs of the teens.

Evaluation

Teenie Boppers was designed as a pilot program, and there are no comparative statistics. Evaluation for the first round of Teenie Boppers was largely anecdotal but included lengthy evaluative discussions with the coordinators of the Young Mothers Program. Additional statistics include attendance

numbers and the number of books made available to the teens during the program.

This program has some specific issues that affect the statistics, particularly the attendance numbers. These issues include the following: (1) Students at Sem Yeto High School decide when they would like to attend school and (2) Many of the women in the Young Mothers Program are in the late stages of pregnancy, and medical concerns prevent them from attending class.

The founder of the Young Mothers Program attended session 4. She observed the entire program and personally thanked the young adult librarian for facilitating this program. She commented that the girls need to build positive relationships within their communities. The girls, while sometimes hesitant at first, always participated enthusiastically in the discussions, even asking for more specific details (for example, asking for more specifics on a certain scholarship program or for books by a specific author). Even after the end of the program's first semester, the anecdotes continue. Recently, one of the Young Mothers Program coordinators brought several of her students into the library to check out books. She stopped by the reference desk and again thanked the young adult librarian for instituting the Teenie Boppers program.

Relevance to Overall Young Adult Services

Young adult service at Fairfield Civic Center Library utilizes the approach known as youth development. Programs offered by the branch include a teen book club, Dance Dance Revolution tournaments, Warcraft III tournaments, volunteer opportunities (including a docent program in which teen volunteers help children learn how to use the computer), information literacy, computer, and craft programs. Youth development seeks to "make an affirmative impact" on the lives of teens and, in turn, positively affect the communities they serve. The after-school programs, such as the Dance Dance Revolution tournaments, seek to provide a healthy activity and the opportunity for teens to have their own space. Teenie Boppers offers something in the same vein: The opportunity for teen mothers, who are usually responded to negatively, to realize that they have a say in what services the library offers. They become aware that someone else in the community wants to see that they succeed.

Each of the programs in existence at Solano County Library and the Fairfield Civic Center branch utilizes the input of teens. Teens asked for more computer classes, so the 2007 Summer Reading Program includes four. Teen volunteers provide invaluable input in terms of collection maintenance and development and truly work with the library.

These programs, including Teenie Boppers, provide positive programming for and with teens. Programs stem from the particular interests of the young adult librarian and the needs of the local teen community.

Teenie Boppers Storytime

STORYTIME AGENDA

Topic: _____

Opening Song (1): _____

Song (2): _____

Longest Book: _____

Song (3): _____

Book: _____

Fingerplay (4): _____

Song (5): _____

Book: _____

Closing Song (6): _____

--- SAMPLE STORYTIME ---

Teenie Boppers Storytime

Topic: Counting

Opening Song (1): *Itsy Bitsy Spider*

Song (2): *Five Little Ducks*

Longest Book: *Ten in the Den*

Song (3): *Name Song*

Book: *The Balancing Act*

Fingerplay (4): Wiggle

Song (5): *Twinkle Twinkle*

Book: *Click, Clack, Splish Splash*

Songs and Fingerplays

Closing Song (6): *If You're Happy and You Know It*

Opening Song (1) : *Itsy Bitsy Spider*

The itsy bitsy spider
Went up the water spout.
Down came the rain
And washed the spider out.
Out came the sun
And dried up all the rain.
And the itsy bitsy spider
Went up the spout again.

Song (2): *Five Little Ducks*

Five little ducks went out one day.
Over the hills and far away.
Mama Duck said
Quack, quack, quack
And four of the little ducks
Came back.

Repeat using 4, 3, 2, 1

Sad Mama Duck went out one day.
Over the hills and far away.
Mama Duck said
Quack Quack Quack
And all of the little ducks came back.

Song (3): *Name Song*

Baby's Name over the water
Baby's Name over the sea
Baby's Name catches a favorite color bird
But you can't catch me!

*Go around the entire circle and get each
baby's name.*

Fingerplay: *Wiggle*

Wiggle fingers.
Wiggle toes.
Wiggle shoulders.
Wiggle nose.

Repeat at least once

Song (5): *Twinkle Twinkle*

Twinkle Twinkle little star.
How I wonder what you are.
Up above the world so high.
Like a diamond in the sky.
Twinkle Twinkle little star.
How I wonder what you are.

Closing Song (6): *If You're Happy and You Know It*

If you're happy and you know it
Clap your hands.
If you're happy and you know it
Clap your hands.
If you're happy and you know it
Then your face will surely show it.
If you're happy and you know it,
Clap your hands!

*Repeat with kick your legs, beep your nose,
wave bye bye.*

Living in a Diverse World

Teenie Boppers Teen Time

Introductions

The basics of storytime

Age based needs

Storytime

Teen Time

Sharing of books

Next month's topic: Careers

Assignment: In the next session the library staff will talk about one book you have read for yourself and one book you have read to your child. Please be prepared to say a little bit about both books.

Assignment for Next Session: _____

_____

_____

The Book I Read for Myself

Title: _____

Author: _____

What I Thought About the Book: _____

_____

The Book I Read to my Child

Title: _____

Author: _____

What I Thought About the Book: _____

_____

What I thought about reading the book to my child: _____

_____

Teenie Boppers Teen Time

TEEN TIME AGENDA

Storytime

Teen Time

Next month's topic: _____

_____

Assignment: _____

_____

_____

Assignment for Next Session: _____

_____

_____

five

Living in a Diverse World

The description for this category is services or programs to teens that promote respect for differences and reach out to teens of diverse backgrounds, such as ethnicity, language, sexual orientation, learning and communication styles, gender, disability, or economic status. YALSA is very much committed to bringing more diverse professionals into the profession and to provide tools for members to serve diverse teens. In 2007, YALSA was awarded a grant from the American Library Association's Ahead to 2010 Initiative to launch a major, multi-year diversity campaign. During the first year, YALSA sponsored a Spectrum scholar and developed diversity programs for conferences. The campaign will have many exciting new directions in future years. The following four programs are also excellent examples of programs that celebrate diversity in young adults.

Top Five Program

TITLE OF THE PROGRAM/SERVICE

International Teen Club

Hennepin County Library, Minnetonka, Minnesota

Type of program/service:
Series/ongoing program/service

Targeted audiences:
Senior High, At Risk, New Immigrant

Name of contact person:
Nong Lee, nlee@hclib.org

Other categories:
Creative Teen Clubs, Community Connections, Reading Raves

Program Summary

The International Teen Club (ITC) is a youth involvement group located at the Brookdale Library, one of forty-one within the Hennepin County Library (HCL) system. The mission of ITC is to engage Hmong youth in creating programs for other Hmong youth at the library and exposing them to a positive environment while maintaining their Hmong roots. The goals of the program are to encourage youth leadership, community involvement, asset building, and lifelong learning. ITC meets every Monday evening, in addition to other evenings and weekends for special events. Like all youth involvement groups, attendance varies, but there is a strong core group of fifty Hmong teenagers who are primarily high school students. ITC seeks to actively engage its teen members in constructive activities. It began in 2004 with the recruitment of volunteers at high schools.

Description of Library

The Brookdale Library is one of the largest libraries (62,000 square feet) serving the northern suburbs of the Minneapolis. It is one of forty-one libraries in the HCL system. HCL's mission is to promote full and equal access to information and ideas; the love of reading; the joy of learning; and engagement with the arts, sciences, and humanities. The work is built on a foundation of eight core principles.

1. HCL services and facilities respond to a changing and growing population.
2. HCL facilities are gathering places.
3. HCL is committed to children, teens, and families.
4. HCL engages and serves seniors in accessible settings.
5. HCL leads in technology.
6. HCL facilities are designed and constructed to be flexible and sustainable.

7. HCL is a judicious steward of the public's financial investment.
8. HCL values partnerships that contribute to county and library goals.

Intended Audience and Demographics

The program targets Hmong youth ages 12 to 18, living in the cities of Brooklyn Park, Brooklyn Center, and Minneapolis. Students come from five different school districts. Participants are the children or grandchildren of first generation Hmong immigrants who primarily came to the United States in 1980s. The Hmong population in the Twin Cities is the largest in the United States with many families living in the northern suburbs.

Rationale

ITC is important because it engages Hmong youth in positive activities that build assets. Some ITC activities include: knitting club, flute class, poetry slams, creative writing workshops, poetry publication, kite making workshop, field trips, author visits, cultural celebrations, fashion shows, talents shows, DVD production (from developing storyline to script writing to shooting and editing video), volunteer parties, karaoke contests, Dance Dance Revolution, and other tech programs.

As these activities illustrate, ITC is built on the other core values outlined in *New Directions for Library Services to Young Adults* by Patrick Jones (ALA 2002) focusing on outcomes for teens. ITC is an example of a library working with teens, not for teens. In ITC, teens are treated as individuals, not stereotypes.

Planning for ITC began with staff reviewing the development assets model from the Search Institute. Many of the activities address these developmental assets. Activities such as breakdancing, Dance Dance Revolution, and karaoke allow teens to move around! Activities such as the knitting project and flute class let members learn, practice, and demonstrate new skills.

ITC members see themselves as both library users and supporters, representing the library in community events such as the Hmong New Year celebration held annually at the Metrodome in Minneapolis. Programs such as the creative writing workshops, the poetry publication, and DVD production allow creative teens to show off their talents. Because these young people come from different school districts, they are given a chance to make new friends, as well as see adults and library staff in a new light. From volunteering and working with younger children to representing the library at community events to publishing their own poetry to creating a DVD to promote the library, ITC moves Hmong teens from passive library customers to active community contributors. ITC members have advocated for their program before the Brookdale Library Friends and through the ITC DVD, which promotes library use to teens, new immigrants, and members of the Hmong community. Partners in programs have included Park Center High School, the Minnesota Humanities Commission, and Hmong's Women's Circle. The library has conducted information literacy workshops for ITC members, as well as engaged them in to contributing to the library's Web page (www.hclib.org/teens) through podcasts, and creating media. Book discussion groups (with occasional author visits), poetry slams, writing workshops, and the ITC poetry publication all have promoted reading among ITC members. ITC is a model for the library's developing after-school homework help program aimed at increasing student achievement.

Number of Young Adults Reached

Average attendance at most events is thirty. Attendance is higher at program such as the Hmong cultural celebration, where hundreds attend, including relatives of ITC members.

Number of Staff and Volunteers

ITC is primarily the work of Hmong outreach liaison Nong Lee. On average, Nong dedicates two to eight hours per week on ITC projects. He is assisted by youth librarians from the Brookdale Library. Volunteers are not used in ITC, other than the ITC members themselves, who volunteer hundreds of hours for the library.

Funding and Budget Figures

The funding for staffing derives from the personnel budget of the Hennepin County Library with an estimated $3,000 spent annually ($20 per hour times an average of three hours a week for fifty weeks). Programming is funded through the Library Foundation of Hennepin County. Funding varies annually but in recent years, the Foundation has supplied $5,000 to fund all other aspects of the program, such as funding books for book discussion, hiring performers, author honorariums, and creating ITC T-shirts.

Marketing

As a standing program, the ITC recruitment is done primarily through word of mouth. Special programs such as the Hmong Cultural Celebration or poetry slams, are marketed through the library's program guides, flyers, posters, as well as on the library's Web site.

Youth Participation

Opportunities for youth participation run throughout ITC. More than just developing ITC activities, the ITC members actively engage in other projects such as working with Hmong children, sorting materials for book sales, and assisting in developing of the TeenLinks Web page. ITC members have even participated in the Hmong

National Conference as volunteers or hosts through the library, as well as volunteering for the metrowide teen summer reading kickoff. They've done everything from suggesting materials for the library to purchase to helping choose furniture for the revamped Brookdale teen area.

Evaluation

The primary evaluation of ITC is ongoing attendance at the biweekly meetings, and attendance at special events. All ITC members get library cards, although circulation is not tracked. A survey capturing attitudes of ITC members was conducted in 2005 and in 2007. Perhaps the best evaluation of ITC is the Hennepin County Library's new after-school program, as well as youth participation groups at other libraries that were all inspired by the ITC model. Other libraries could start a similar culture-based club based on populations of ethnic or immigrant groups in the area, such as Asian, Indian, or African American.

Relevance to Overall Young Adult Services

As noted, the ITC is the model for newly forming teen programs, including another group aimed at Hmong teens, one focusing on other Asian teens, and one reaching out to Latino teens. Facilitator Nong serves on the system's teen services team that conducts programs all year, but focuses on summer programs, Teen Tech Week™, and Teen Read Week™.

Resources

Benson, Peter L., Pamela Espeland, and Judy Galbraith. *What Teens Need to Succeed: Proven, Practical Ways to Shape Your Own Future* Minneapolis: Free Spirit Publishing, 1998.

Braun, Linda W. *Technically Involved: Technology-Based Youth Participation Activities for Your Library* Chicago: ALA Editions, 2003.

Jones, Patrick, Michele Gorman, and Tricia Suellentrop. *Connecting Young Adults and Libraries: A How-to-Do-It Manual For Librarians* (How-to-Do-It Manuals for Libraries, No. 133). New York: Neal-Schuman, 2004.

Jones, Patrick and YALSA. *New Directions for Library Service to Young Adults*. Chicago: ALA Editions, 2002.

Tuccillo, Diane. *Library Teen Advisory Groups: A VOYA Guide*. Methuen, N.J.: Scarecrow Press, 2005.

AnimeCon

Louisville Free Public Library, Louisville, Kentucky

Type of program/service:
Single program/special event

Targeted audiences:
Middle School, Junior High, Senior High

Name of contact person:
Kate Schiavi, kate@lfpl.org

Other categories:
Special Events

Program Summary

AnimeCon is an annual event where teens (ages 12 to 19) gather at the Louisville Free Public Library (LFPL) main library to celebrate all things anime. The convention was originally conceived because of the overwhelming interest LFPL teen patrons had for anime and manga. Several branches had organized monthly anime clubs, and manga was one of the highest circulating materials among teens. The anime revolution was certainly taking over the library and AnimeCon was developed in response to that. Over the past three years, AnimeCon has developed from a small four-hour program into a full two-day event that more than five hundred teens attended in 2006. In addition to anime screenings, the 2006 convention featured workshops focusing on Japanese culture, writing and drawing for manga, teen-led panel discussions, and a bookmobile filled with nothing but manga and anime.

Steps

Below is the timeline the library staff followed in planning the August event.

January

- Begin anime convention proposal
- Begin to formulate outline of possible events
- Discuss possible workshop facilitators

February

- Continue revising proposal
- Contact other libraries that have hosted similar anime events for tips

March

- Finish proposal and budget and submit to administration
- Contact possible workshop facilitators
- Seek out donations from anime companies for giveaways and door prizes
- Contact Community Relations about anime exhibit and gallery spaces
- Devise anime artwork guidelines for the gallery exhibit

Reserve meeting rooms

April

- Finalize workshop facilitators
- Investigate costs for the Dance Dance Revolution game
- Start considering new anime releases to screen at the convention
- Promote anime artwork exhibit among branches and notify branch staff of the guidelines for artwork submissions
- Promote anime artwork exhibit to anime library clubs

May

- Continue to seek anime artwork submissions
- Begin accepting artwork to be included in the exhibit
- Create anime trivia game to be played at convention

June

- Meet with workshop facilitators to finalize workshop outlines and plans
- Create promotional flyers and send to library branches to be displayed
- Submit teen artwork to community relations for anime exhibit
- Decide on anime titles to screen and obtain permission rights from company
- Create convention evaluation to be handed out to participants

July

- Submit information to community relations for inclusion in the August/September monthly calendar
- Order supplies in-house
- Go shopping for other necessary supplies
- Continue to market program to anime clubs and in the branches.
- Start registration for convention

Description of Library

The Louisville Free Public Library system in Jefferson County, Kentucky includes a main library, sixteen branches, and three bookmobiles. An additional satellite branch is the Young Adult Outpost, which is a library space dedicated to serving teens. LFPL serves metro Louisville with a population of nearly 700,000 people. The main library, which hosts the annual AnimeCon, is situated in downtown Louisville in the historic Carnegie Library built in 1908. Approximately 400,000 people visit the main library annually. In 2007, the library partnered with Jefferson County Public Schools to issue each student a new library card. As a result of this program, all teens in public schools were issued a new library card.

Intended Audience and Demographics

There were two specific audiences targeted for AnimeCon 2006: The two-day event was for teens, ages 12 to 19 and another half-day program was for children ages 5 to 11. The 2000 census reports that the teen population in Louisville was 168,271. Of this, 77.4 percent were identified as Caucasian, 18.9 percent as African-American, 1.8 percent as Hispanic/Latino, 1.4 percent as Asian, and .5 percent other.

Rationale

AnimeCon strives to encourage teens' interest in anime and manga. This event gives young adults the opportunity to socialize with peers who share similar interests; offers reluctant readers a chance to have literary experiences; allows teens to express their creativity through art, writing, and costume making; and provides teens with a sampling of Japanese culture. AnimeCon has also broadened the awareness of anime and manga in the Louisville community as evidenced by the number of newspaper articles surrounding the event.

Number of Young Adults Reached

The estimated daily total of teen participants for AnimeCon 3 was 250. Over the two day period, the convention hosted approximately 500 participants.

Number of Staff and Volunteers

Two co-coordinators (Kate Schiavi and Kerry Hunter) spend approximately sixty hours planning the program (developing the schedule, updating the Web site, coordinating and developing workshops, meeting with workshop facilitators, speaking at meetings about the event, promotional time, and shopping for supplies and prizes). Staffing the two days of the event included eight staff people for eight hours a day (totaling sixteen hours per staff member). Additional staff planning for workshops totaled approximately eight hours.

Funding and Budget Figures

This program was funded by the library's yearly children's programming budget. The total amount spent was approximately $700. With more than 500 participants at the program this breaks down to about $1.40 per person. The following is a breakdown of budgetary costs:

Purchases

Dance Dance Revolution game pads	$120
Plastic holders for name badges	$100
Prizes for cosplay and door prizes	$100
Craft materials and origami paper	$125
Foam board for signs	$30
Miscellaneous costs	$50

Workshop Facilitators/Performers

Yumi Nagaki, Japanese tea ceremony	$85
Graham Shelby, Japanese storytelling	$95
Marty Edlin, MetroArts Center (services exchange with Metro agency)	*Free*
Louisville Kendo Club	*Volunteered services*
Louisville GO Club	*Volunteered services*

Marketing

The library's graphic artist designed the AnimeCon 3 poster, which gained recognition among both teens and adults. The convention was marketed at each branch with the display of the AnimeCon 3 poster and a feature article was included in the library's newsletter. Much of the interest in the convention was generated among the teens and their word-of-mouth communication. Some local anime clubs mentioned Anime-Con on their electronic discussion lists or Web sites. The event was also covered in several local newspapers, including the *Louisville Courier-Journal*.

Youth Participation

Youth participation is integral to AnimeCon's continued success. Suggestions and comments made by teens in the monthly anime clubs have enhanced the convention over the past three years. The 2006 convention featured six sessions developed and led by teens. These included panel discussions, anime trivia, and an origami workshop. One of the most popular components of the convention is the art exhibit that features anime-style artwork submitted by local teens. The art is displayed throughout the duration of the convention for participants to enjoy. Teens also volunteered on the days of the convention to help with registration, setting up meeting rooms, and crowd control.

Advertising for AnimeCon 3

Evaluation

The success of AnimeCon is evident by the number of participants each year. The first year the event was a half-day program that attracted close to one hundred teens. The second year of Anime-Con was a full day event that approximately two hundred teens attended. The convention in 2006 was a full two-day event with two hundred fifty teens each day. Many participants attended both days of the convention. Statistics have also shown that as a result of AnimeCon, the attendance at the monthly branch anime clubs has increased and more branches are offering anime-related programs.

Each year participants are asked to fill out evaluation forms at the conclusion of the convention. The responses are essential to the planning process for the next convention. Some of these responses follow:

After two full days at the Anime Convention this weekend, Taylor came away with a brighter than average smile. She has often felt a little outside the loop, thinking very few people shared her interest. This weekend really blew her mind and she felt a wonderful sense of camaraderie for the first time. As her parents, it was really exciting for us to see her make that connection. This poster will be a wonderful reminder for her. The library staff feel fortunate to have such a bountiful and diverse public library in Louisville. Thank you for all your hard work!—Ann, mother of AnimeCon participant

The gallery was a really good idea because most people don't acknowledge anime as a real art form. Also, cosplaying was neato! —Sarah, participant

In response to the evaluation question: What was your favorite part of the convention?

The drawing session: the artist who taught it gave me good pointers on drawing my character. I don't draw and he gave me confidence in my attempt.—Anonymous participant

AnimeCon speaks to an interest that teens already have, and appeals to a ethnically and gender-diverse crowd. The event builds interest in reading manga and other young adult literature. It also introduces or expands on an interest in Japanese culture

Planning time is essential. For the program to run smoothly (like a real convention) planning for all the little details is essential. Finding ways to involve the teens in running workshops or volunteering at the event is a great way to get them excited about it.

Staff encountered a few glitches during the process: not enough planning time, not coordinating the schedule well, having too much down time between events (it is important to always have something going on), and making sure the Ramen Noodle eating contest is in a place where clean up is easy and the teens can be loud.

At another library, this two-day event can certainly be scaled down. The first year the library staff did it, it was a four-hour program where the library staff showed an anime video and had a few activities. Or it could be spread out to different branches so that all the branches were to offer some type of anime-related event throughout the course of a week or two.

Relevance to Overall Young Adult Services

The anime convention has become the basis for the development for teen programming at LFPL. The convention grew out of the response to the popularity of anime-related programming offered at nearly half of the library's branches. Due to the success of AnimeCon, system-wide teen programming has become a major component of LFPL's service to young adults, and it has become the model for how teen programming continues to develop at LFPL.

Resources

Ideas for sessions: www.animeboston.com

Ideas of anime to show and prize support: www.funimation.com

Ideas of anime to show: www.bandai-ent.com

Ideas of anime to show: www.advfilms.com

To purchase DDR games: www.ddrgame.com

Daily schedule of events: www.lfpl.org/teenpages/ animecon.html

Outreach to the Crossroads Youth Opportunity Center

Prince George's County Memorial Library System, Hyattsville, Maryland

Type of program/service:
Series/ongoing program/service

Targeted audiences:
Middle School, Senior High, At Risk, Families

Name of contact person:
Myra Katz and Kelli Kanvin,
myra.katz@pgcmls.info

Other categories:
Community Connections, Reading Raves

Program Summary

At the request of the Office of Youth Strategies and Programs of Prince George's County, the Prince George's County Memorial Library System (PGCMLS) developed outreach services to the Crossroads Youth Opportunity Center, a free and confidential program that offers services to at-risk 12- to 17-year-olds in a region of the county where gang participation is high. A two-part strategy was implemented: First, a small lending library was established for the teens and their families, and then events and programs were planned and continue to run.

Steps

The first component was the lending library. PGCMLS agreed to establish a small lending library that would house books, magazines, and library information. Library staff installed permanent shelving in the waiting room and lounge area of the Crossroads Youth Opportunity Center.

After meeting with a group of the teens and their counselors for input on specific subject areas, the outreach librarian put together a collection of books and other materials to suit their needs. Because the majority of those using the center are native Spanish speakers, materials were supplied in both English and Spanish. All books are available for browsing as well as check out. Users may check out the material using a simple sign-out honor system since both the library and the center wanted to keep procedures easy and straightforward. PGCMLS staff monitor the collection and send fresh and current library promotional material. A library from a bordering county also supplies books for the collection.

The collection includes both new and used books and three magazine subscriptions. In addition, new titles for the collection were purchased with funds supplied by the library's community partner, the Office of Youth Strategies and Programs of Prince George's County. The collection contains approximately 450 to 500 books to support both informational and recreational needs.

Areas of the collection include:

- fiction and poetry titles for teens;
- nonfiction titles for teens in areas such as photography, drawing, computers, sports, fashion, sexuality and pregnancy, history, and science;
- magazine subscriptions, including one newsweekly and one Spanish-language weekly;
- nonfiction titles for parents, particularly in the area of self help; and
- fiction and nonfiction for children of all ages (for siblings and family reading).

For the programming component, the PGCMLS outreach specialist assigned to the Crossroads Center project did an initial presentation on library services, including information on the databases and on Tutor.com, a live online homework service available from their facility via the library Web site. At that time, the teens were asked about their interests to plan future programming.

An outreach specialist, hired specifically to work with teens, was added to the team working on the project and a summer book discussion series was planned to be held on five consecutive weeks. At the completion of the series, the program would be evaluated and future plans made.

Suggestions were solicited from the counselors at the center for the type of material to use. They preferred that the literature relate to street and gang issues. As the program proceeded, it was clear that expanding the scope was desirable.

Because this was a targeted audience, there was no formal promotion, but the staff at the center was absolutely essential in promoting the program with their clients. The intent of this discussion was not to be an extension of school with assignments and judgmental evaluations. There were no attendance requirements. Seating was informal; teens sat on bean bag chairs, couches, and each other. While there was a set time to begin, latecomers were welcomed as a number of the attendees used public transportation or came from a job. The sessions were planned and structured, yet informal, which allowed for a relaxed atmosphere and free flow of ideas.

Attendance grew and many participants attended multiple sessions, but attendance was not consistent from one week to the next. While aiming for continuity from session to session, it was very important that each program was able to stand on its own.

Participants were given a journal for writing and drawing. It was made clear that these were for their private use; they were not expected or required to share.

Each of the sessions lasted from an hour to an hour and a half. The components of each were:

1. *Opening activity.* An interactive icebreaker of some kind was introduced. For example, one week a series of "What would you do?" situational ethics questions were presented. These, and other activities, are easily found online or in books. The first week, participants were hesitant to share opinions and needed gentle prodding. They loosened up considerably by week five.

2. *Literature presentation.* Books or photocopies of individual stories or poems were handed out to each member of the group. Poetry was read aloud at the first two sessions, short stories at the rest. While it was planned for the teens to do the reading aloud to the group, most were hesitant to do so because of literacy or language issues. Therefore, facilitators did most of the reading as the teens followed along, which they did with amazing interest and dedication! Discussion followed the readings. It was important to give them some time to digest and gather their thoughts about the posed questions.

3. *Audiovisual activity.* This crucial element to the program, which varied from week to week, added variety, addressed different learning styles, and helped keep interest. This element does not necessarily have to

tie in to the literature. The following were used with success: music, DVDs, PowerPoint presentation, short movies, photography, and flip charts.

4. *Refreshments.* Chips, candy, soda, and pizza were popular.

Description of Library

PGMCLS is a suburban public library that serves a population of more than 800,000 residents in a jurisdiction that borders Washington, D.C. Sixty-eight percent of the county's population is African American; 12 percent is Latino; and 20 percent is Caucasian. The library, which has 324 salaried employees and 100 hourly employees, operates eighteen branches plus service outlets in the County Administration Building and the County Correctional Center. In its six large branches, PGCMLS provides service through separate age-level departments for adults, young adults, and children; small and medium branches are staffed by generalists.

A great deal of age-level training is provided to both generalists and specialists, and cross-training among age-level departments is encouraged.

Intended Audience and Demographics

A specific teen population was targeted for the program. At the request of the Prince George's County Office of Youth Strategies and Programs, PGCMLS developed outreach services to the Crossroads Youth Opportunity Center. The center was formed as a result of a bicounty task force on gang violence and is a free and confidential program that offers services to at-risk teens and their families in a region of the county where gang participation is high. The teens that use the center range in age from 12 to 17 and are exclusively Latino and African American. They have been identified as potential gang members and are thus eligible for the services of the center, which include one-on-one mentoring; job training and placement; individual, group, and family therapy; legal support and representation; and recreational needs. The collection of the lending library was established to meet the needs of the families of the teens as well as of the teens themselves.

Rationale

Having come from cultures where public libraries are not readily accessible, many of the clients of the center have no experience with libraries. Consequently, the ability to borrow books is seen as an extraordinary treat. A recent emigrant from Mexico, an enthusiastic reader, was thrilled to learn that she could borrow books; she had never been able to have books at home. She eagerly borrows books to read aloud to her little sister as well. The area where Crossroads is located is sufficiently distant from library branches, and public transportation is difficult for teens to navigate or too costly. This increases the importance of the lending library in a facility where the teens visit for other purposes—for example, counseling, mentoring, recreation, and so on. A discussion of library services introduced the teens to various ways in which they could use the book collection and online resources available through onsite computer stations to help with school work.

This also served to inform the teens about the concept of public libraries with the hope that when they are able to use a public library branch, they will be more inclined to do so.

The book discussion group is meant to encourage meaningful discourse by the teens through the introduction of accessible and engaging literature that will help them develop literacy and communication skills.

Number of Young Adults Reached

The potential audience is approximately 120 teens although more than 200 have gone through the Crossroads program from its inception. Statistics are not kept on the number of teens who borrow materials (as the honor system is employed), but it is the counselors' opinion that many of the clients—the teens and their families—either borrow books for home use or find time to read or browse through the books and magazines at the center. A group of teens and their counselors were involved in the planning of the lending library.

Number of Staff and Volunteers

The library director and associate director for public services were involved in the initial negotiations with the Office of Youth Strategies and Programs and the Crossroads Center staff to establish a partnership. Previously, a neighboring library system had left a small collection of materials, but the officials of the center were interested in having more appropriate shelving, a more targeted collection, and some ancillary services established for the at-risk population that uses the center. When the preliminary plans for the partnership were complete, the library's outreach specialist was introduced to the project, and she performed all of the tasks needed to get the collection and services established. Recently, an outreach specialist, hired specifically to work with teens, was added to the team working on the project. She is working closely with the original staff member; they will work collaboratively on the collection maintenance and on presenting the book discussion program. As time goes on, the original staff member will turn over primary duties to the teen outreach specialist and will help with the project on an as-needed basis.

Staff time needed for the lending library included installation of shelving by the maintenance mechanic for one day. Initial selection, ordering, processing, delivering, and set up of the collection took forty to fifty hours time by the outreach specialist.

Each programming session required six to eight hours for planning. Two staff members facilitated each of the discussions.

Funding and Budget Figures

PGCMLS provided an initial collection of books and magazines, including both new and used books and three magazine subscriptions. The value of the new books, which were mostly gift copies that the library did not purchase, was $900; the subscriptions cost $81.91. In-kind donations ($1,375.39) included shelving and the labor to install the shelving (at an estimated cost of $192.12). Staff time of the outreach specialists is estimated to have cost approximately $1,450. This represents forty to fifty hours spent placing orders, processing materials, delivering and setting up the collection, and time spent at the center in programs and meetings.

The Office of Youth Strategies and Programs provided funds for new books at a cost of $674.40 and for posters to decorate the area around the collection at a cost of $34.

Cost of support materials and refreshments for the five-week discussion series was approximately $140 in real dollars and $50 in-kind. This office also agreed to pay for events planned for future months.

Marketing

No external marketing was done by the library as the center targets its service to a specific clientele. Within the center, the lending library is prominently located in the reception area, and the counselors bring attention to the materials and the ability of center users to borrow from the collection. The counselors also personally promote the presentations and programs.

Youth Participation

Approximately eight teens were involved in providing feedback for use in program planning and collection development. Similar meetings with teens will be held on a semiannual basis so that as new clients come into the program, their reading needs can be considered.

Evaluation

While there was a small lending library in the center prior to this partnership, anecdotally, the counselors reported that few materials were borrowed or read. Since the borrowing is done according to an honor system, there are no statistics on usage. This was done intentionally to demonstrate to the teens that they were trusted at the center. The Office of Youth Strategies has indicated that it is not concerned that all materials be returned as the at-risk teens served at the center would benefit from books in the home. The project director and youth counselors have reported that both teens and their families are using the collection. This is evidenced by the need for additional materials and the general disarray found when they were delivered. The homework help presentation was the first ever at the center so there are no comparable figures.

The strength of the program was engaging a population that traditionally does not know the extent to which the library can help serve their needs. It is hoped that the lending library will not only supply needed books and so on, but will support the idea of a public library as an institution that can be counted on for service.

In just a few short weeks, the book discussion series, began a trust that allowed for a powerful expression and exchange of ideas via poetry, story, and discussion. Spanish was the first language of many of the participants. The activities allowed them to foster their English-language skills. Establishing a successful format for the book discussions—one that can be replicated, fostered, and enhanced, was achieved.

Initially, it was not apparent that each program should stand alone. Facilitators found that they could not count on participants returning each week having read an assigned book or story. That became clear when on the second week there was only one attendee from week one. Others from week one returned on subsequent weeks.

Literature and other material had to be selected that could be presented and discussed within the same session while allowing for members to continue on their own, if they wanted. Having the same staff present the programs made for continuity and familiarity, even over a short period of time, which led to trust and better discussions. Having two facilitators worked well. It is useful to remember that some material works better than other material, and that some discussions are more dynamic than others. As ever, it is critical not to underestimate the members of the discussion group.

The lending library could be replicated on a smaller scale by establishing a small deposit collection in a recreation or community center, counseling office, family shelter, or other place where hard-to-reach teens and their families might spend time.

The program can be held at a variety of venues—the public library, a school library (lunchtime or after school), a recreation or community center, a counseling office, or family shelter. It could easily be adapted to a specific age range or might be offered only for teen girls or boys. The discussions should take place weekly and can focus on a particular theme or not. If possible, partner with another community organization with programs for youth or a public or independent school and informally survey the group to assess their needs and interests. Holding the program at the center allowed for discussion of material not necessarily appropriate for a school or public library. Mature themes and subject matter were discussed freely, with the pre-approval of the center counseling staff.

Relevance to
Overall Young Adult Services

PGCMLS has operated with a strong young adult services service plan over many decades, with great respect for teens' unique informational, educational, and recreational needs. With this project, the library staff also recognizes that at-risk populations, such as those who live in the service area of the Crossroads Center, have unique challenges to fulfilling their informational needs. Among these are lack of accessibility to public library facilities, language barriers, and a strong gang culture in their surroundings.

Many of the clients of the Crossroads Center have serious problems that are addressed through counseling, mentoring, and reading; books and cultural activities often take a back seat to more systemic problems. Yet, many of the teens are pleased to have access to materials they could not find in their school libraries and to which they do not have access at home. The lending library and the programs presented by the outreach librarians contribute, in a small way perhaps, to the teens' information literacy, their appreciation of literature, and their learning and achievement. They help fulfill the library's goal of providing age-appropriate, culturally sensitive materials for teens in the formats and languages with which they are comfortable.

Resources

(for sample programs on pages 86–87)

Def Poetry Jam: Season 3. Dir. Stan Lathan. Perf. Russell Simmons, Mos Def. DVD. HBO, 2005.

Didato, Salvatore. *The Big Book of Personality Tests: 100 Easy to Score Quizzes That Reveal the Real You*. New York: Black Dog & Leventhal Publishers, 2003.

Forbes, Jack. "Only Approved Indians Can Play: Made in USA." *Prejudice: Stories About Hate, Ignorance, Revelation, and Transformation.* Daphne Muse, ed. New York: Hyperion Books for Children, 1995.

The Lottery. Dir. Larry Yust. Videocassette. Encyclopedia Britannica Films, 1969.

Myers, Walter Dean. "Monkeyman." *145th Street: Short Stories*. New York: Dell Laurel-Leaf, 2001.

Peck, Richard. "Priscilla and the Wimps." *Sixteen: Short Stories by Outstanding Writers for Young Adults*. Donald R. Gallo, ed. New York: Bantam Doubleday, 1984.

The Rose That Grew From Concrete, Vol. 1. CD. Interscope Records, 2000.

Rosen, Michael. *Michael Rosen's Sad Book.* Cambridge: Candlewick Press, 2005.

Shakur, Tupac. *The Rose That Grew From Concrete.* New York: Pocket Books, 1999.

Sheindlin, Judy. *Judge Judy Sheindlin's Win or Lose by How You Choose!.* New York: Cliff Street Books, 2000

Kickoff

I. Introduction

    a. Welcome

    b. Explanation of book discussion program

    c. Icebreaker

II. Tupac Shakur as musician (question and answer format)

    a. Find out about group familiarity with Tupac

    b. Did you know . . . (interesting facts about Tupac)

III. Tupac as writer/poet

    a. Hand out copies of *The Rose That Grew From Concrete* by Tupac Shakur

    b. Discuss format and history of the book

IV. Poetry v. Rap

    a. Discuss differences

    b. Read, interpret, and discuss several poems from the book (Facilitator can start this process and then encourage participants to read or select subsequent poems.)

    c. Compare with musical interpretations on *The Rose That Grew From Concrete,* Vol. 1 CD

V. Watch selections from *Def Poetry Jam* DVD

VI. Wrap-up

    a. Final thoughts

    b. Hand out journals for participants to write their own poetry, rap, or other forms of expression

Sample program from Crossroads Youth Opportunity Center Outreach Program

SAMPLE WEEKLY PROGRAM

I. Introduction

    a. Welcome

    b. Explanation of book discussion program (for new and returning members)

II. Icebreaker: Situational Ethics

    a. Participants choose from among cards prepared ahead, each containing an ethical dilemma (A balance of serious and light-hearted works well.)

    b. Encourage nonjudgmental discussion

III. Short Story

    a. Hand out copies of "Monkeyman," a short story from *145th Street: Short Stories* by Walter Dean Myers

    b. Read aloud and discuss

IV. Iconic Photographs: PowerPoint presentation

    a. Present photographs spanning the 20th Century featuring powerful social imagery

    b. Have brief background material on each photograph

    c. Solicit feedback on date, subject matter and personal reactions

V. Wrap-up

    a. Final thoughts

    b. Hand out journals to new participants

Cultural Heritage Series
for Young Adults

**West Covina Library, a County of Los Angeles Public Library,
West Covina, California**

Type of program/service:
Series/ongoing program/service

Targeted audiences:
Middle School, Junior High, Senior High, International

Name of contact person:
Monique Delatte, teenboard@gmail.com or mdelatte@gw.colapl.org

Other categories:
Community Connections, Services Under $100, Special Events

Program Summary

At the West Covina Library, a County of Los Angeles Public Library (CoLAPL), the Young Adult Board is particularly interested in understanding the multicultural community of Los Angeles. In 2006 and 2007, the library staff have hosted YA celebrations (and follow-up sessions for staff) of African American, Chicano, Creole, East/South Indian, Chinese, and Filipino cultures.

Steps

Chinese Cultural Heritage Day

ONE MONTH IN ADVANCE

Funding. Raise money for the event by working directly with the Friends of the Library, community groups (such as Chinese American associations) and through grants and library funds. The Young Adult Board cultural heritage series is funded through the generosity of the Friends of the West Covina Library,

the County of Los Angeles Public Library, the Arcadia chapter of the Chinese American Human Service Association, and private donors.

Marketing. Advertise the event at least three weeks in advance. Publicize programs through booktalking and information literacy sessions in schools, the city and library Web sites, local teen organizations, and local newspapers and radio stations. Young Adult Board members may be interested in promoting the event at city council meetings with staff. Word of mouth is best, so passing out flyers everyday to young adults who are already in the library is more good advertising.

Planning. Involve the teen volunteers in planning the event. The chief accounting officer of the Young Adult Board created Web pages through which other teens could sign up to volunteer for the event. Several volunteers wrote and performed plays about the origin of the Dragon Boat and Mid-Autumn festivals.

In total, twenty volunteers and thirty-five to forty participants enjoyed the celebration.

TWO WEEKS IN ADVANCE

Hunting and Gathering. Shop for decorating supplies in Chinatown or at party supply stores. Red envelopes are available, at no charge, at most Chinese American banks. In Chinese tradition, red envelopes are filled with a monetary gift; you can use certificates for the Friends of the Library book sale or video rentals. The library staff supplemented the supply of free bank envelopes with Ellison Dye envelopes (dye #17769) that the library staff decorated with golden dragons (dye #13148) and fish (dye #13302). Additionally, teens made one hundred hanging paper lanterns with red construction paper, scissors, and a stapler. To replicate these, simply cut slits in a piece of construction paper (leave an inch uncut at the top and bottom), then staple the paper at both ends into a tube shape, and staple a paper handle on top (5″ × 1″). Hang from the handle.

ONE OR TWO DAYS IN ADVANCE

Shopping. Gather provisions, preferably at a market catering to an Asian American community, with the coworker who will be helping the young adults prepare the dishes. Sharing the planning process with colleagues spreads goodwill, reminding staff that inviting teens into the library is rewarding. Purchase moon cake, tea, and dumpling and egg or spring roll ingredients.

Decorating. Set up the event area with booths signifying various Chinese cultural events or crafts. The library staff decorated tables to recognize the New Year, Mid-Autumn, and Dragon Festivals. Also featured were beading, lantern-making, and calligraphy stations and food and drink areas. The New Year booth featured red envelopes, and the Mid-Autumn booth offered delicious moon cake samples.

Imaging. Develop and hang a sign that recognizes your sponsors. Accent booths with large, attractive signs. (Staff found an accordion paper dragon to visually identify the Dragon Boat booth, and faux firecrackers for the New Year booth.)

ONE DAY IN ADVANCE

Cooking Class. Teach the young adults how to prepare the dishes to be steamed or fried the next day. A page who had emigrated from China shared this facet of her culture with the teens.

Prepping Food. Assist the young adults in preparing about eighty of the dumplings and egg or spring rolls in advance (remember to include vegetarian options). These will be steamed or fried at the Chinese Cultural Celebration. The aroma will tantalize every family in the library!

DURING CHINESE CULTURAL HERITAGE DAY EVENT

Demonstrating. Assign young adults to demonstrate how to wrap and roll Chinese culinary delights. An adult should fry or steam the treats. In charge of the fryer was a lively Filipina librarian (the cultural culinary palette of the Philippines includes dishes of Chinese origin).

Staffing. Station two volunteers at each booth, although three or four teen volunteers may be needed to keep the cooking demonstration booth moving at the pace of demand.

Welcoming. Arrange for two young adults to greet visitors, armed with informational literature. The Young Adult Board chief executive officer and chief operating officer were in charge of welcoming families (and staff).

Performing. Break twice for dramatic performances celebrating Chinese American festivals.

Recording. Snap oodles of pictures, and share the camera with teens.

Cleaning. Remind volunteers to help clean and break down the event area.

Evaluating. Rate the program by following the event with a brief Young Adult Board meeting wherein attendees offer verbal feedback and complete short evaluation forms. Speak informally with attendees, their parents, and the staff. Request evaluative comments and suggestions through the Young Adult Board electronic discussion list.

Appreciating. Thank volunteers, process the pictures, and help teens make scrapbooks for and write thank-you letters to sponsors.

Including staff time (two librarians at five hours each and a page at four hours: $260), the total cost was approximately $610.

Description of Library

The West Covina Library is located in eastern Los Angeles County. The population of the county has increased by 4.5 percent from 2000 to 2006. As a county, Los Angeles claims the largest American Indian/Alaska Native population, at 156,000. Also residing in this county are the largest populations of Latinos (4.5 million) and Asians (1.3 million). Los Angeles County also claims the greatest numerical increases for these groups from 2000 to 2003: Latinos (of any race) at 300,000 and Asians at 47,000. At 2.7 million, Los Angeles County holds the largest population of children. It is very important to CoLAPL to provide opportunities for these young people to learn about their culture and the cultures of their peers.

Intended Audience and Demographics

The specific audience includes any 12-to 18-year-old who is in interested in participating.

West Covina is a diverse city. According to the 2000 census, the population is approximately 46 percent Latino, 44 percent Caucasian, 23 percent Asian, 21 percent other, 7 percent African American, and 1 percent Native American—one-third of the population is foreign-born. Interestingly, more than half of West Covinians speak a language other than English at home. It is relevant to note that 28.5 percent of the population is under age 18, a number that is 1 percent greater than California as a whole.

Rationale

Young adult services at West Covina Library that focus on cultural connections provide targeted learning opportunities for teens and tweens. Homeschoolers and students from local middle and high schools are then able to interact with adult presenters and teens in a meaningful way—wrapping saris, enjoying Dragon Boat Festival theater, tasting Chicano treats, or crafting a Filipino Christmas star. The employees of the library are also pleased to share their cultural heritage with the young adults. For example, Chinese and Filipino employees taught teens how to prepare egg rolls and dumplings for the Chinese Cultural Heritage Day event.

Number of Young Adults Reached

In adding up the attendance at these events, and accounting for repeat visitors, the YA Board cultural heritage programming series has included some 250 young adult participants.

Number of Staff and Volunteers

The programs have involved approximately thirty staff members and one hundred volunteers, of all ages. The event generally becomes a party for the staff as well as the teens. (In fact, many staff members are teens. An event such as Kwanzaa allows the staff to enjoy the tradition of cooking and sharing soul food together.)

Funding and Budget Figures

The YA Board cultural heritage programming series has been funded by CoLAPL, the Friends of the West Covina Library, the Arcadia chapter of the Chinese American Human Service Association, and by smaller donations. Figures listed here are per event.

The YA Board Indian Cultural Heritage Celebration on May 30, 2006, required $300 in performer fees for two hours of mehndi artistry. Two employees hosted the event. Several hours were spent planning, shopping for supplies, and executing the program. The cost to CoLAPL of staff time was approximately $20 per hour for one librarian (five hours) and $24 per hour for the second librarian (four hours). The performer provided the henna for mehndi tattoos, the library staff provided Indian snacks (under $30) and saris (no cost), which one staff member wrapped around the teens in the traditional style. Staff greatly enjoyed sharing their cultural history with the young people. The total cost was about $525. Volunteer teens helped with set up and clean up. They also maintained a waiting list, cueing teens when it was their turn.

Chinese Cultural Heritage Day was sponsored by the Friends of the Library ($150) and by a generous $200 donation from the Arcadia chapter of the Chinese American Human Service Association. Including staff time, the total cost was approximately $610.

The Young Adult Board celebrated Filipino culture by creating traditional Filipino Christmas star lamps, in front of the West Covina Library. Each Filipino star lantern took about two hours to construct. To prepare the craft, four volunteer teens began by bending and gluing wood into a star shape, then adding a paper-mâché cover to the dozen lanterns. Young adults then met after school to decorate the stars using glitter, paint, markers, and crayons. The event cost approxi-

mately $50 in Friends of the Library monies. Including staff time, the program was $180, as two staff members worked for a total of six hours.

The Kwanzaa celebration featured a poetry class and reading by poet, Tajii Simone ($40, sponsored by CoLAPL). Volunteers decorated the meeting room using black, red, and green bows and origami. Informational literature was provided to attendees, as was a poetry newsletter produced by Simone ($10 printing cost to CoLAPL). Following the reading, approximately thirty guests enjoyed soul food from Hungry Al's Barbeque, including saucy ribs and delicious collard greens ($200 total). For dessert, the teen crowd gobbled peach cobbler, red velvet cake, and assorted pastries prepared by library staff and patrons. The Friends of the Library sponsored this educational and fun celebration of African American culture. A library aide and assistant dedicated several hours to assisting with Kwanzaa preparations, so the combined labor cost was about $170, making the total cost approximately $420.

The library initiated a new year of young adult programming with a visit from Filipina author Melissa de la Cruz. Teens enjoyed baking brownies for guests. The cost of employee labor was approximately $80 for four hours of time. The brownie supplies were about $20, making the total cost $100.

For Throw Me Somethin', Mister! The Young Adult Board celebrated on Fat Tuesday with king cake, throws, and music tracks by the Mambo Kings. The party was paired with a rigorous Princeton Review SAT prep session. The program had twelve attendees, including two parents and one sibling. The king cakes were mailed to the library from Louisiana, as a gift from the librarian's mother and the Princeton Review program was complimentary. The only cost was the cost of staff time for three hours, or $60. On his evaluation form, Devin A. wrote, "It was helpful to learn about test scores."

Cinco de Mayo was celebrated on International Worker's Day in front of the library with Mexican snacks, such as pan dulce, and Aztec-inspired airbrush tattoos. The cost of the per-

Beading Booth at Chinese Cultural Heritage Day

Making dumplings for Chinese Cultural Heritage Day

former was $150. The cost of the food was under $20. One employee assisted with the purchase of the treats and combined with the librarian time, the cost of labor was $80. The total cost was approximately $250.

Marketing

To market these events, flyers were delivered monthly to ten local middle and high schools. Events were also publicized through the city, county, and library Web sites and the local papers. The librarian also promoted events by speaking at West Covina City Council meetings and local meetings, like those hosted by the Chamber of Commerce. Programs were also promoted through booktalks and information literacy sessions at the schools, as well as at other school events, such as registration day, career day, volunteer day, and parents' night.

Youth Participation

Young adult programming began with the arrival of librarian Monique Delatte in 2005. Cultural programming followed in the spring of 2006. Teens helped with every cultural event, from providing input about cultural celebrations, but also with marketing, set up and clean up. They were also instrumental in designing matching decorations for each event to go up in the library, further promoting the series. Their influence was celebrated in every detail of the programs.

Evaluation

To evaluate each program, the librarian holds brief YA board meetings directly after the events. Attendees also offer verbal feedback and complete short evaluation forms. Staff solicits further informal feeback from the attendees, their parents, and other staff. Evaluative comments and suggestions are also solicited through the YA electronic discussion list. Kwanzaa evaluation form comments included: "Very well presented," "It was very good and I enjoyed it—very educational. I hope to see this happen next year."—A., "Very good, I loved it," "It was great participating and learning about other cultures. It should be done more often!" and "Thank you. It was very educational."

Another issue came up when the YA Board decided to host Chinese Cultural Heritage Day at the end of the summer. The only problem with this timing was that it did not overlap with the Mid-Autumn festival, so moon cakes were expensive and difficult to find. Other libraries eager to offer their own cultural festivals should be aware that certain foods and supplies may be available only seasonally.

Relevance to Overall Young Adult Services

Celebrating cultural heritage and creating an atmosphere of inclusiveness are two benefits of the YA cultural heritage series that concurrently benefit library staff. CoLAPL young adult services is supportive of programs that engender greater acceptance of teens in the library. Penny Markey, youth services coordinator, has written, "The library provides an annual summer reading program as well as an array of programs for children and families throughout the year to support reading, learning, and multicultural understanding." Welcoming teens is a priority at CoLAPL, and multicultural programs provide an excellent opportunity to invite young adults to participate in library activities.

Resources

Anderson, Sheila B. *Extreme Teens: Library Services to Nontraditional Young Adults.* Englewood, CO: Libraries Unlimited, 2005.

Booth, Heather. *Serving Teens through Readers' Advisory.* Chicago: ALA Editions, 2007.

Dresang, Eliza T., Melissa Gross, and Leslie Edmonds Holt. *Dynamic Youth Services through Outcome-Based Planning and Evaluation.*Chicago: ALA Editions, 2006.

Jones, Patrick for Young Adult Library Services Association. *New Directions for Library Service to Young Adults.*Chicago: ALA Editions, 2002.

McGrath, Renée Vaillancourt. *Managing Young Adult Services: A Self-Help Manual.* New York: Neal-Schuman, 2002.

Nichols, C. Allen, ed. *Thinking Outside the Book: Alternatives for Today's Teen Library Collections.* . Englewood, CO: Libraries Unlimited, 2004.

Young Adult Library Services Association, Renee Vaillancourt McGrath, ed. *Excellence in Library Services to Young Adults: The Nation's Top Programs,* 4th edition. Chicago: ALA, 2000.

Vaillancourt, Renée J. *Bare Bones Young Adult Services: Tips for Public Library Generalists.* Chicago: Public Library Association and Young Adult Library Services Association, 2000.

Additional Resources for Young Adult Librairans

WEB SITES

Books for the Teen Age, New York Public Library: http://teenlink.nypl.org/bta1.cfm

YALSA's Booklists and book awards: www.ala.org/yalsa/booklists

Nancy Keane's booktalks: http://nancykeane.com/booktalks/ya.htm

VOYA booklists: www.voya.com/WhatsInVoya/booklists.shtml

DATABASE

NoveList: Young Adult Level Booktalks, Browse
  Lists

NEWSPAPER

Teen Ink

MAGAZINES

RHI: Reaching Reluctant Readers Magazine
Newtype:USA
Teen Voices

RADIO

Youth Radio: www.youthradio.org

six

Services Under $100

While this description is pretty clear, the application for this category celebrates unique initiatives that offer high impact services or programs that are low in cost. With shrinking budgets, there is no school or public library that does not need more inexpensive program ideas!

Top Five Program

TITLE OF THE PROGRAM/SERVICE

Teen/Senior Web Connection

Alameda County Library, Fremont, California

Type of program/service:
Series/ongoing program/service

Targeted audiences:
Senior High, Intergenerational

Name of contact person:
Gary Morrison,
gmorrison@aclibrary.org

Other categories:
Teen Tech Week™, Community Connections,
Living in a Diverse World

Program Summary

The Teen/Senior Web Connection program serves the needs of both teens and seniors. It provides the ability for teens to earn volunteer credits and learn teaching skills by tutoring seniors on how to use the Internet. Teens receive orientation and training, and are then matched one-on-one with seniors wanting to become comfortable with the Internet.

The program evolved from a desire to offer teens a meaningful way to earn school-required community service hours with a need to help the older adult patrons become familiar with the Internet. These seniors, many of whom had Web access at home, had little idea how to actually use online resources. They wanted to communicate by e-mail, but they didn't know how to begin setting up an e-mail account. They had basic information needs, but didn't know how to go about performing basic searches.

Steps

The teens go through an orientation and training before they are assigned a senior. In general, they meet with the senior about an hour a week, until the senior feels comfortable using the Internet. For some seniors, that may be three or four sessions, for others it may be six or more. The trainings always occur at the library. Once a teen/senior pairing has ended, the teen is then assigned the next senior on the waiting list.

Description of Library

Fremont Main Library, the largest branch of Alameda County Library, serves a city of 211,000, with about 10,000 high school students, and 32,000 adults over age 55.

Intended Audience and Demographics

The program is aimed at students enrolled in high school, as well as senior citizens in the City of Fremont. The diversity of Fremont is significant, in that the large Asian, Indian, and Afghani populations total 37 percent of the city population. Both the participating teens and seniors in the program reflect this demographic.

Rationale

The importance of the program is signified by the opportunities it provides for teens to earn volunteer credits by assuming the role of teaching, while providing a much needed service to seniors.

The teens gain an understanding of the role of teaching, a skill not often gained in many traditional volunteer roles. And, they often start to understand the information needs of a segment of the community that may have previously seemed far-removed from their own. They may not realize their importance in "bridging the digital divide." Teens and their parents have mentioned that when joining the program they were somewhat apprehensive as to how they would interact with the seniors. In virtually all cases, they have been very successful, and some have continued in the program even beyond their service hour requirements.

Many of the seniors have tried the local adult schools and senior centers, but have been frustrated by the classroom approach to teaching the Internet skills they need. The seniors are very appreciative of the teens (and the library) for providing this setting, where they can learn in a one-on-one environment.

Number of Young Adults Reached

The library recruits for the program two or three times per year, depending of the number of teens in the program and the number of seniors on the waiting list. At any given time, the library staff may have six to ten trained teens, and ten to fifteen seniors waiting to be tutored.

Number of Staff and Volunteers

The training is done by two staff members, the teen librarian, and the senior services librarian. It is a three-hour training, in which teens are given an understanding of the library's role in teaching information-seeking skills, patron confidentiality, referring reference questions, and working with issues often relevant to seniors, such as physical limitations. Frontline staff are responsible for signing in teens, who record their service hours.

Funding and Budget Figures

The actual cost of the program is limited to producing, in-house, the flyers and application brochures for the program, which varies on the needs for teens and their senior counterparts, but is typically less than $50. Staff time for the three-hour training sessions is not included as it is part of the programming already in the job description for those two librarians.

Marketing

The program was promoted to teens, primarily through flyers and application brochures made and distributed in-house, and also via local high schools. School librarians, counselors, teachers, and administrators were also a conduit. Press releases in the local media were also utilized. To reach seniors, flyers were also distributed to senior centers, retirement centers, and the local adult school. Many of the seniors became involved through referrals of frontline staff, in the course of helping them with computer-related questions at the reference desk.

Youth Participation

Although library staff took the lead role in developing the program, they relied on the teen volunteers for feedback on the viability of the program. Teens expressed the rewards of working with seniors, with some minor frustrations on the logistics of arranging times for their sessions. Usually it was the seniors who, for medical and personal reasons, had to cancel meetings on short notice. Each training session held included teens from the previous group, who answered questions and helped respond to anxieties of incoming volunteers.

Evaluation

Although there has been no formal evaluation, feedback from both teens and seniors has given every indication that the program is successful. Teens and seniors have told staff repeatedly that any minor apprehensions they had entering the program were replaced by strong feelings of accomplishment and self-esteem.

Relevance to Overall Young Adult Services

The program directly addresses the mission of the library: "The Alameda County Library system provides and protects access to books, information and services that promote learning and enjoyment for everyone." In keeping with the overall mission of the library, teens learn the importance of information literacy by realizing that there is a segment of their community that needs extra attention to develop skills required to achieve necessary computer competencies. The Teen/Senior Web Connection has benefited the teens and the seniors in the community and further enabled the library to serve an important role by providing a program that allows them to work together in such a positive environment.

Teen/Senior Web Connection

SCHEDULING

1. Look at the days and times your senior can meet, and compare with your own busy schedule.

2. Choose a few possibilities of days and times that work for both of you.

3. Call your senior and discuss when to meet.

4. Try to agree on two or three sessions and schedule them together.

5. Tell your senior that you'll call him/her the day before each meeting as a reminder.

6. Call the library (745-1444) to reserve an Internet Station for your meeting. Be sure to tell the librarian that you're a tutor for the Teen/Senior Program.

7. Make sure your senior knows how to contact you in case they can't make the meeting.

YOUR FIRST SESSION WITH YOUR SENIOR

1. Try to arrive five minutes early to check in at the reference desk, get your badge, and log your hours.

2. Introduce yourself to your senior. Shake hands if you're comfortable doing that.

3. Ask your senior how they want to be addressed, for example, Mr. Scully or just John.

4. Find out what your senior wants to learn. Do you feel comfortable teaching those areas? If not, explain other alternatives for them, including referring them to a librarian.

5. Ask them about their experience with computers and the Internet, and what they'd like to learn. Ask them where they'd like to start. Suggest that they may want to take notes to help them practice between sessions.

6. If they've had some experience, have them show you what they can do, so you can see what their level is.

7. If they've had little or no experience, go very slowly. Start by showing them the mouse and how to control it. You may want to point out the mouse tutorials.

8. Have your senior do everything his/her self so they can learn and feel independent.

9. Make sure they understand each step before going on to the next one.

10. Keep checking to make sure you're teaching them what they want to learn.

11. At the end of the session, arrange or confirm your next session. Be sure it's scheduled at the reference desk. Encourage them to practice what they've learned.

12. If they have questions, can they call or email you?

13. Shake hands again. Whew . . . great job!

Tip sheet for Teen/Senior Web Connection

Teen/Senior Web Connection

Working With Seniors . . .

COMPUTER AND INFORMATION NEEDS

Similar as other age groups: _____

____ Entertainment   ____ Communication

____ Health   ____ Economic concerns

____ Family   ____ Travel

____ And more . . .

SPECIAL NEEDS

Mobility: _____

Hearing, vision, and other possible health issues: _____

_____

Unfamiliarity with computers, the Web, etc.: _____

_____

TEACHING TIPS

Patience: Simplify examples, concepts, and definitions

Let the students work the controls.
   Physical issues: Do not grab hand; let student work controls and ask permission
   if it becomes helpful to use the mouse or keyboard. Most folks learn best when
   they get to do things on their own.

Reference Desk: Examples of when to refer questions to librarians.

Confidentiality: Personal, medical, family, etc. Do not share with others.

Teaching Resources: Alameda County Resources (tutorials and other links
   on Web site, books and videos, reference staff, etc.)

ADA Resources: Large monitor and other resources

Outside Resources: Adult schools, senior centers, etc.

Another tip sheet for Teen/Senior Web Connection

Student Novel Nibbles Party

East Jessamine Middle School, Nicholasville, Kentucky

Type of program/service:
Single program/special event

Targeted audience:
Middle School

Name of contact person:
Dorie Raybuck, dorie.raybuck@jessamine.kyschools.us

Other categories:
Reading Raves, Special Events

Program Summary

The idea of Novel Nibbles was to entice students to read a genre that they normally would not choose to read. The library media center (LMC) was decorated with balloons and each of the large round tables was appropriately decorated to represent a specific genre (a vase of roses for romance, and so on); the signage on each table was clear and attractive. Also, the tables held ten to fifteen excellent middle school books from that genre and student response forms. Students learned how to preview a novel and were asked to select three genre tables to browse that they normally would not choose. They then selected a book from the table, previewed the novel, and completed a student response form. Students were allowed to turn in three student response forms for three "goodies."

Steps

Supplies

- Nine colorful tablecloths, one for each table
- Nine stand-up signs for the center of each table

- Giveaways for the "goodies" table (candies, pencils, bookmarks, and so on)
- Good novels from each genre

Set up

- Cover the tables with tablecloths.
- Place the sign and decorations in the center of the table. Be creative! Genre tables can include the following genres: historical fiction, mysteries, horror and suspense, realistic fiction, science fiction, fantasy, sports fiction, or romance.
- Cover the table with good novels.

Directions for Students

- Tell them as a group that they will be traveling to at least three of the eight tables.
- They are encouraged to try "new" genres.
- They are expected to sit at a table and browse the books. After making a selection, they will preview the book and write a student response.
- Tell the students that previewing a book means three things: They must look at the

front cover picture, read the back cover or the inside flap or both, and read the first page of the first chapter.

- Tell students to fill out the student response sheet. They must have one sheet for each genre.

Description of school

East Jessamine Middle School is staffed by fifty-five teachers, of which thirty-three are core content teachers, twelve special education teachers, ten arts and elective teachers, four principals, two counselors, and a school psychologist. Programs range from a special education program to gifted services. The school is currently involved in a national grant program titled Striving Readers involving content literacy. The school utilizes the Accelerated Reader program to promote reading in the school. East Jessamine Middle School has been growing in literacy. This strong reading focus is demonstrated by comprehensive test of basic skills scores, which grew from 51.5 in 2006 to 60.6 in 2007.

Intended Audience and Demographics

The audience consisted of approximately 850 sixth through eighth grade students at East Jessamine Middle School. Students are from various cultures including Mexican, Russian, Ukrainian, Guatemalan, and Costa Rican. Nearly 30 percent of the population has free or reduced lunches. Students live in both rural areas as well as a mid-sized town. The school is located in one of the fasting growing counties in the state of Kentucky.

Rationale

The Novel Nibbles party is one way to promote reading among teens, especially to entice teens to read genres that they would not normally choose

to read. It provides a learning experience in a fun social setting. The LMC space and experience is enhanced for the students, making it a place students like to be and where they will be glad to return. One of the primary goals is to enhance the student-LMC experience to that of visiting a comfortable, social bookstore.

Number of Young Adults Reached

This program reached all 850 students in the school.

Number of Staff and Volunteers

The library media specialist, the library aide, and the literacy and English teachers all collaborated to make this program a success.

Funding and Budget Figures

This program was funded through the library media center budget. There was minimum cost, requiring decorations such as balloons and colorful tablecloths, snacks such as pretzels and bite-sized candies, as well as erasers and other small prizes for the goodies table.

Marketing

The library media specialist advertised the program via e-mail to all teachers, staff, and administrators. The program was promoted during faculty and student meetings, during collaborations with literacy and English teachers, and through signs that were posted throughout the school.

Youth Participation

Early in the school year the library media specialist held a Sip and Browse party for the teachers during a school day. The students immediately asked when a student party was going to happen! This of course was the seed idea for the student Novel Nibbles party. Although students did not participate in preparing for this party, they did initiate the idea and fully participate. Students also evaluated the program in writing and by checking out books in genres they normally would not have selected.

Evaluation

The program was evaluated by attendance, verbal and written confirmations, and of course, by the number of books checked out! This was the first program of this type in the school and planning will continue for future programs.

A possible variation for other schools and even public libraries would be the Sip and Browse teacher or parent party, where new young adult fiction and nonfiction is highlighted by genre or theme.

Relevance to Overall Young Adult Services

One of the primary goals of the middle school library media specialist is to nurture the student-LMC experience. Staff want students to love to be in the LMC, to find comfort, acceptance, information, and learning all in the LMC. The school is about reaching the students in an effective, fun, and nurturing manner. Using student-generated ideas such as the student party idea gives them confidence in themselves as they see how staff respond to their ideas and nurtures the welcoming LMC environment. This momentum will continue with new initiatives based on the positive student and faculty feedback from this one event.

Teen Film Festival:
An Independent View

Livermore Public Library, Livermore, California

Type of program/service:
Series/ongoing program/service

Targeted audiences:
Middle School, Senior High

Name of contact person:
Mary Sue Nocar,
msnocar@livermore.lib.ca.us

Other categories:
Enhancing Teen Spaces, Physical or Virtual,
Community Connections

Program Summary

The Teen Film Festival encourages youth between the ages of 12 and 18 to express themselves through videos. The Teen Film Festival grew out of collaboration between the library, the City of Livermore Economic Development Department, Livermore Area Recreation and Park District, and the Livermore Chamber of Commerce.

Films are critiqued by a panel of filmmakers and producers from the Livermore Valley film community during a Teen Film Festival reception attended by teen filmmakers, families, and friends. The emphasis of the festival is on learning effective filmmaking technique and production. The panel concentrated on what worked and what didn't in each film. Spontaneous conversations occurred between the panel and the teen filmmakers and continued following the program.

Festival films were screened at three additional venues throughout Livermore: Art Walk in downtown Livermore; the Livermore Area Recreation and Park District's Community Center, and during the downtown association's Trick or Treat Night.

Steps

Define the purpose of the festival: Is it a learning experience or to highlight the talent of teens?

Criteria

Next, it is important to establish criteria for the panelists. For this festival, things to think about when establishing the panel include:

- Community members with filmmaking and film production experience
- High profile within the community is a plus
- Good communication and teaching skills especially with teens
- Contact possible panelists by networking within the community
- Contact city departments and agencies, such as the local Chamber of Commerce, for suggestions
- Contact local theater groups and acting instructors

- Do local colleges or universities have a film-making department? Can they offer suggestions?
- Call your local community television station
- Is there a filmmaking group in the area or an annual film festival?
- Plan a date for the library reception/screening and research other venues
- Consider community activities already established—is there a link?
- Besides the library, where and when might the films be screened in the community?
- Again, contact city agencies
- Reserve library venue and arrange for chairs and equipment

Next, criteria needs to be established for film entries and participants (panelists can help develop criteria). Details can include:

- Maximum length of entries, including credits?
- Age and residency of participants
- Whether adults can be involved with any part of the process
- A limit on how many films can be entered by an individual
- Format restrictions
- Requiring mandatory element in each film
- Filmed in a particular location
- Filmed in a certain amount of time
- Requiring a specific phrase in the dialog or a certain image
- Presenting awards for the top films
- Final entry date

Marketing

- Establish a logo, make flyers, design entry form, and list of criteria
- As soon as the date is set, let the middle and high schools know that this event is planned,

and were possible ask to put it on their Web sites and to make announcements.
- Contact local newspapers with a press release (send two—one month before and the other closer to the event).
- See if a local radio station will announce the program.
- Post flyers at the library, other popular teen hangouts, and the schools.
- Put your event on community calendars.
- Get the word out as much as possible so teens have time to make their films.

Technical Support

- Arrange for submitted DVDs to be transferred to single DVDs to be shown in a loop for screenings at the different venues.
- Make certain that various venues have the equipment to screen the DVDs.
- Distribute copies to the different venues for screenings.

Reception/Screening Planning

Give panelists DVD copies of all submitted films one month before the reception. Meet with panelists to plan for the discussion and screening of films: How much time will be spent discussing each film? Will general discussion occur at the end?

If more than eight or nine films are submitted, consider restricting the reception night screening to films that best exemplify filmmaking concepts. Also consider what refreshments will be served. The last step is evaluating the program, either with a prepared survey form for participants and attendees or other methods.

Description of Library

Established in 1878, the Livermore Public Library is supported by the general fund of the City of

Livermore. Located in the eastern portion of the San Francisco Bay area, the library currently provides four points of service. These include a 56,000 square foot Civic Center Library, two branch libraries, and a virtual Web-based library. With up-to-date technology and computer access, the Livermore community has access to electronic and print information and services. Annual use of the library indicates an 11.82 per capita circulation rate and an 8.45 per capita library visit rate. A significant goal in the library's 2006 to 2011 long- range plan is to: "provide programs for teens . . . to reflect and expand their interests," which is mirrored by a portion of the library mission statement which ". . . encourages the development of a lifelong interest in reading and learning by youth and adults."

Intended Audience and Demographics

This festival is intended for Livermore youth between the ages of 12 and 18 years of age. The total population of Livermore is 80,723. According to the Livermore Valley Joint Unified School District, approximately 7,900 youth attend grades 6 through 12 or 9.8 percent of the population. The ethnicity of the students is predominantly Caucasian at 64 percent, with 22 percent Latino and other cultures, including Asian, Filipino, and African American, making up the population.

Rationale

The Teen Film Festival is important because it brings community agencies together to support and foster the talents and interests of local teens. The ability, imagination, and ingenuity of the teens are open for all in the community to acknowledge and appreciate. Teens develop problem-solving skills, plan career paths, and reinforce positive relationships during interaction with adult filmmakers. The equality and ease of

the interaction and the lack of pressure to win, as no awards are given, provide an encouraging environment. This opportunity to showcase talents validates them as individuals and contributing community members.

Number of Young Adults Reached

Eleven young adults submitted films to the Teen Film Festival in 2006, the first year. The festival reception and panel discussion drew ninety-two people. A high percentage of the audience included the young filmmakers and their friends. Families, teachers, and city agency employees also attended. An estimated 30,000 members of the community and visitors viewed some or all of the festival films at the various venues.

Number of Staff and Volunteers

Seven people were directly involved in the program. One library staff member planned the program and contacted members of the community and city staff for support. A city staff member from the Economic Development Department collaborated with the library to network within the community and other city agencies to assist with marketing. Five filmmakers and producers from the community donated their time previewing the films, planning, and participating during the reception discussion. Approximately four additional city and library staff assisted during the evening of the reception and screening, making printed marketing materials and providing technical assistance.

Funding and Budget Figures

Staffing included two librarians, two city partners, and technology support for a total of forty-nine hours at a cost of $1,531.07. Those costs were shared by the supporting agencies, and programming is already under the job description of the librarian. Materials were very inexpensive, costing the library only $25 as the city partners paid for the 1,000 quarter sheet flyers. This program is in the category of Services Under $100 because materials for the program cost $25. Staffing figures were not counted towards that status.

Marketing

Marketing was a collaborative effort with each of the following agencies contributing: Livermore Area Recreation and Park District, Livermore Chamber of Commerce, Livermore Department of Economic Development, Livermore Downtown, the Livermore Public Library, and the TriValley Artists Guild. Program information was posted on local high school, library, and city agency Web sites. News releases were sent to the media including radio stations. Posters and flyers in English and Spanish were distributed to local business, posted in public display kiosks, and available at public libraries. Program information was listed on community calendars and listed in area recreation guides.

Youth Participation

During the initial planning for the Teen Film Festival, teens were consulted about its feasibility, structure, and parameters. Once the films were submitted, their contents dictated the focus and scope of the panel discussion. Questions from the teen filmmakers following screening of each film directed the subject topics discussed. A survey was distributed to all those who attended requesting an evaluation of the program and suggestions for improvements.

Evaluation

This was the first time the program was presented. The program evaluation forms that were returned were very positive. Multiple verbal accolades for the program were received as were recommendations for improvements for the following year. The filmmaker/producer panel felt the program was very successful and most plan to return as panel members.

It is important that the festival criteria be clear to both the entrant and staff members. Determining where one can be flexible within concern to the entries is also beneficial. The first years of the program may only produce a handful of entries. If the library criterion for entry is set in stone, one may end up without a festival.

Other libraries would even expand the program by giving awards and putting on a real awards night where teens can come dressed to the nines and walk a red carpet.

Relevance to
Overall Young Adult Services

The library has celebrated the individuality, creativity, and perspective of young adults in the community for the past three years with the Teen Art Expo. This program encourages Livermore residents in grades 6 through 12 to submit a piece of original art, visually expressing a distinct perspective on life in Livermore now or in the past. The Teen Art Expo experienced a 292 percent increase in attendance from 2006 to 2007. The Teen Film Festival was a natural extension of this very popular program.

OFFICIAL ENTRY FORM

@ the livermore public library: teen film festival: An Independent View

Please use this form for all submissions. Use one form for each submission.

TITLE OF FILM_____

PRODUCER/DIRECTOR_____

CONTACT PERSON_____

ADDRESS_____

TELEPHONE_____

E-MAIL ADDRESS_____

SUBMISSION TYPE(CHECK ONE):
___Live Action (narrative or documentary using real people/actors)
___Animation/Experimental (any animated film or film without a traditional story line.
___Music Video (using images to the music of a single song or a video or a live band performance.)

FORMAT: All entries must be on DVD.
RUNNING TIME: Films must be no longer than 5 minutes in length.
HOW DID YOU HEAR ABOUT THE TEEN FILM FESTIVAL?
_____

PLEASE PROVIDE A BRIEF SYNOPSIS OF THE SUBMITTED DVD:
_____
_____
_____
_____
_____

LIVERMORE
CALIFORNIA
LIVERMORE PUBLIC LIBRARY

Entry form for Teen Film Festival

Flyer for Teen Film Festival

seven

Special Events

The category of Special Events covers a program or service that runs no more than twice a year and that has high interest or high impact on area teens. Some employ more than one category from the Excellence initiative, as in the case of the Year of the Teen in Monroe County, Michigan. The others are indeed unique of other categories while still employing the Excellence spirit as seen in all the programs in this collection.

TITLE OF THE PROGRAM/SERVICE

2007: Year of the Teen

Monroe County Library System, Monroe, Michigan

Type of program/service:
Series/ongoing program/service

Targeted audiences:
Middle School, Junior High, Senior High

Name of contact person:
Paula Loop, paulaloop@monroe.lib.mi.us

Other categories:
Enhancing Teen Spaces, Physical, or Virtual;
Creative Teen Clubs; Community Connections

Program Summary

The Monroe County Library System (MCLS) designated 2007 as the Year of the Teen. The campaign slogan for this project is "Make Yourself Heard @ the library," and fits perfectly with the library objective of giving a voice to teens. With the formation of a teen advisory group and a logo contest for teens to design and choose along with their new name, library staff hoped to show the teens in the community that the library listens to them. By providing teens with a positive space, staff hoped to show teens what a great resource the library can be.

The program started with the formation of the Teen Services Committee (TSC) in the fall of 2006. The TSC started planning a series of monthly events geared toward teens ages 13 to 19. New programs were developed such as Openground, where the main branch is open only to teens one Friday a month 6 to 10 p.m. Because there is no teen space in any of the branches, this is a great way to offer teens a place where they can feel free to talk, socialize, and have access all the library's resources in a teen-friendly atmosphere. More than seventy to eighty teens come in during the four-hour period to check books and movies out, use the computers or gaming equipment, do homework, and just have fun at the library. With other programs like Arts after Dark (performance art showcase), Afterschool @ Bedford, Open Play Gaming, anime events, and Pizza and Pages book group, a good variety of monthly events for local teens are provided.

Description of Library

The Monroe County Library System serves all of Monroe County, Michigan, with sixteen branches. The mission is to enrich the quality of life for all residents of the county by providing free access to informational, educational, and recreational resources. The main branches

Promoting The Year of the Teen

are Ellis Reference and Information Center and Bedford Branch Library.

Intended Audience and Demographics

Programs serve all teens ages 13 to 19. As of the 2005 census, there were 152,392 people in Monroe County. Of that number, 24.2 percent are in grades 9 through 12. The programs bring in teens of many ethnicities and income levels.

Rationale

Teens in Monroe County need a place, outside of school, where they can develop their social, leadership, artistic, and intellectual skills in a healthy and supportive environment. Staff felt that teens in the community do not realize what a great resource the library can be, and may not always feel welcome at the library.

When staff started adding teen programs at the main branches, the teens were surprised by all the "stuff" available. Most did not realize that the library carries graphic novels, young adult books, and even gaming equipment at some events. They also didn't know that library cards are free, that they can search the catalog and reserve online, or have input on teen materials and programs. Now teens realize that the library is there for them, for whatever they need.

The library is quickly becoming the last totally free resource in the community, and the teens should be taking advantage of it. While staff makes flyers that advertise events, the best advertising comes from the teens themselves who go out there and talk about the great time they had at the library. That underlines the need for this initiative and how well it was received.

Number of Young Adults Reached

The monthly regular programs and special events both bring in a steady number of teens. For exam-

ple the Openground program draws between sixty to eighty teens over a span of four hours. A concert with local bands kicked off the teen logo design contest, which had more than two hundred teens in attendance. The quarterly Arts after Dark programs are the most popular and bring in approximately 150 teens. During the first half of the Year of the Teen, more than 2,500 teens attended programs.

Number of Staff and Volunteers

Five active members of the Teen Services Committee started this initiative in January 2007. The committee met weekly for two hours to discuss and evaluate the programs, plan for the special events and discuss the minutes from the Youth Advisory Board that meets monthly at the Openground program. Members also take turns devoting time to work events along with volunteers. During a busy week with multiple events, there could be anywhere from six to ten hours of event time with at least two staff members at each event. Slower weeks might require only a few hours of work at events.

The Youth Advisory Board usually has roughly fifteen to twenty members in attendance at the monthly meeting. They also volunteer at the larger events, and help plan and keep events in touch with what teens want. The library staff also has reference and circulation staff members of the Ellis branch help out at the Openground events to be able to provide complete library services to the teens. MCLS presented eighty-five teen programs from January 1 to June 1, 2007.

Funding and Budget Figures

When this initiative was first conceived, there was no more funding available in the current budget for more teen events. The Teen Services Committee used a few hundred dollars from the building programming budget to begin. Because this is a budget used by all departments for programming, this was not a good long-term solution.

Staff began to work with local organizations and businesses in the community to further extend the reach of events. Jimmy John's sponsored the Openground programs by providing free food to the teens. Mancino's Pizza sponsored the Pizza and Pages monthly reading group by providing free pizza. The Youth Advisory Council of the Community Foundation of Monroe awarded the library a grant in the amount of $3,600. Local bands contributed their time to play at the logo contest kickoff concert. The library paid four bands $75 each from the grant money to cover the cost of gas and equipment.

Marketing

Monthly flyers and posters are displayed at the library that list all the teen events happening that month at the different branches. Staff made a display at the high school and the volunteers and Youth Advisory Board members hand out flyers at their schools. The library has a redesigned teen page on the Web site and has added MySpace, YouTube, and Flickr pages. E-mails and MySpace bulletins are then sent when special events are coming up. Staff has met with representatives from the local high and middle schools to discuss the programming and each school is sent current activity information and publicity materials. The best form of advertising comes from the teens themselves spreading the word to all their friends about what a great time they had at the library.

Youth Participation

A Youth Advisory Board meets at the Openground event every month. There are usually fifteen to twenty members who attend regularly. One of the Teen Service Committee members moderates the meeting and discusses new ideas and upcoming events and how to make them "teen friendly."

Teens are also informally consulted about events and services at all programs. New events, totally conceived and planned by the teens are being developed. The teens are very eager to participate and volunteer to help with any of the events.

Evaluation

Staff members maintain a variety of use statistics to compare with previous years. Attendance records are kept, and evaluation is solicited not only from the youth board, but the attendees of the programs as well. Staff compiled quotes and video testimonials of what the teens think of the new programming. Prior to this initiative, the few programs offered for teens were not drawing a very large attendance. At the Bedford Branch, where staff was complaining of having teen issues and discipline problems, a decline in these occurrences was seen as teen programming increased.

Relevance to
Overall Young Adult Services

This new initiative has created a more comprehensive program of young adult services throughout the library system and has energized young adult services to a higher level. Young adult services have expanded from a few teen activities to a long-term commitment to programs, services, and opportunities for teens at the Monroe County Library System. By involving more teens, getting them into the branches, and encouraging them to use the resources, teens are now using the library and are leaving happy.

Resources

Library Web site: http://monroe.lib.mi.us/ the_scene/main.htm
MySpace: http://myspace.com/clubellis
YouTube: http://youtube.com/mclsclubellis
Flickr: http://flickr.com/photos/clubellis

Greater Rochester Teen Book Festival

**Monroe County Library System, Fairport Library Council and
Fairport Central School District, Fairport, New York**

Type of program/service:
Single program/special event

Targeted audiences:
Middle School, Junior High, Senior High,
Intergenerational, At Risk

Name of contact person:
Stephanie Squicciarini, ssquicci@libraryweb.org

Other categories:
Community Connections

Program Summary

The Greater Rochester Teen Book Festival (TBF) is a free, daylong event held at Fairport High School in Fairport, New York. Young adults are given the opportunity to interact with a variety of authors who write books specifically for a teen audience. The day begins with a keynote speech and informal question and answer session with all of the speakers. Each author then presents three workshops, known as "breakout sessions," in which they talk about writing and answer questions. Teens have the option to attend sessions for three different authors. Between workshops, participants may eat lunch, listen to music performed by teen bands, and browse the book sale area operated by an independent bookseller. There is a special autographing session during the last hour and a half so that teens can meet and have personal interactions with the authors.

Steps

The first step was to form a committee with cross-representation from school and public libraries.

This committee created a mission statement and goals for the TBF and formed subcommittees for the major tasks involved. Subcommittees included fund-raising, Web site creation and maintenance, author hospitality, volunteer coordination, and publicity. All components of the TBF are then conducted simultaneously, with the first year taking a full sixteen months to plan and the second taking eleven months. The fund-raising committee sought partnering sponsors and developed fund-raising efforts that included Read-a-Thons, bottle and can drives, and official TBF merchandise sales. These fund-raising efforts are ongoing and continue year-round to help create a foundation on which to build future TBF events.

Negotiations for honoraria, expenses, and other details are finalized with either the authors directly or with their representatives. The schedule of the day is finalized, with each author presenting three times, each for about thirty to forty minutes.

Teen entertainment is sought, with local bands and DJ clubs starting off the day and performing during lunch and the closing autograph session.

Description of Library

TBF is a cooperative venture between the member libraries of the Monroe County Library System, the Fairport Library Council, the Fairport Central School District, and several other schools in the greater Rochester area. The Monroe County Library System provides service to Rochester and Monroe County residents. It consists of the Rochester Public Library, ten city branches, and twenty town libraries. The Fairport Library Council facilitates communication between all public, school, and special libraries in the Fairport Central School District. With two middle schools, a dedicated ninth grade school, and one high school, the Fairport Central School District enrolls a total of 4,156 students in grades 6 through 12.

Intended Audience and Demographics

In 2005, there were 85,848 students enrolled in grades 6 through 12 in Monroe County, New York. About 78 percent are Caucasian, 14 percent are African American, 5 percent are Latino, and 3 percent are of other ethnic backgrounds.

Rationale

The TBF was an opportunity to dedicate an event to teens that would both encourage and celebrate their reading and demonstrate their value to and within the society. Other community members such as public and school librarians, graduate and undergraduate college students, and parents are also invited to attend but teens are given preferential seating during breakout sessions. The entertainment during the day is also selected with teen interests in mind. Meeting authors they admire can make a lasting impression on teens, possibly encouraging them to become authors or follow their own dreams.

In the past years the planning committee has also encountered a few parents who have mentioned that reading a particular author's books meant so much to their teen that it saved him or her from suicide. Stories like this remind everyone involved with TBF why this event is so powerful and must continue.

Number of Young Adults Reached

In 2006, there were five hundred estimated attendees, and in 2007, the number increased to one thousand.

Number of Staff and Volunteers

The 2007 planning committee, chaired by Stephanie Squicciarini, teen services librarian at the Fairport Public Library, was comprised of fifteen members, including eight school media specialists and seven public librarians, representing five school districts and three counties in the region. The fifteen-member planning committee enlisted the services of forty-two teen volunteers and twenty-eight adult volunteers, for a total of eighty-five people running the festival. The committee met monthly over the course of eleven months, and sometimes bimonthly, for roughly two hours each time. The in-kind services of the fifteen participating libraries totaled five hours per week per staff member during the eleven months.

The day of the festival includes fourteen hours. The total estimate, including all work needed to plan and execute the festival, is roughly four thousand hours, not including the volunteers on the day of the festival.

Funding and Budget Figures

Costs of the festival vary depending on the number of authors and their travel expenses. The total cost estimate based on the opening two years of the festival is approximately $15,000. This included ten to twelve authors (honoraria, travel, and lodging), dinner events before and after the festival, office supplies, volunteer T-shirts, and start-up creation costs of TBF merchandise to sell before and during the festival.

Teen Book Festival Expenses

Author honoraria and travel	$12,072.39
Meals and hotel	$2,961.26
Festival merchandise	$2,843.22
Supplies/decorations	$438.72
Building usage fee	$365.73
TOTAL	$18,681.32

Teen Book Festival Income

Tops/Martins Supermarkets	$1,000
Lift Bridge Books (20 percent of proceeds from festival sales)	$1,250
Fairport Central School District	$10,250
Friends of Libraries in Monroe County	$4,100
PTSA group	$1,050
Rochester Area School Librarians Professional Association	$750
Honeoye Falls-Lima High School	$2,000
Fundraisers	$4,548.35
Merchandise sales	$4,199.32
Proceeds from 2006 TBF	$3,415.16
Private donations from individuals	$375
TOTAL	$32,937.83

Trifold brochure advertising the Teen Book Festival

Marketing

Marketing for TBF was largely a grassroots effort. The committee followed the traditional route of newspaper press releases, library displays, and flyers. Authors and libraries linked their Web sites directly to the festival Web site to reach the online community. Principals and superintendents in each school district in Monroe County and surrounding areas received fliers and personal invitations to attend TBF. Whenever possible, the local PTSAs publicized the event in their electronic and paper newsletters.

Fund-raising helped immeasurably in spreading the word about the event. Students at nine public and school libraries held read-a-thons. Another fundraiser, called "Cans in a Cooper vs. Bottles in a Beetle," was picked up by two local television newscasts. Students at Martha Brown Middle School in Fairport had a competition among the grades to collect the most bottles and cans. They ultimately gathered eleven thousand and then experimented with whether they could fit more cans in a Mini Cooper or bottles in a Volkswagen Beetle. Proceeds from the deposits on all of the recyclables were put towards TBF expenses. Merchandise such as dog tags and tote bags with the festival logo were also sold in advance as a form of free publicity. Many members of the libraries' Teen Advisory Boards purchased these items for interested friends.

Youth Participation

Young adults played an integral role in making TBF happen. Planners with Teen Advisory Boards often brought ideas to their meetings to get

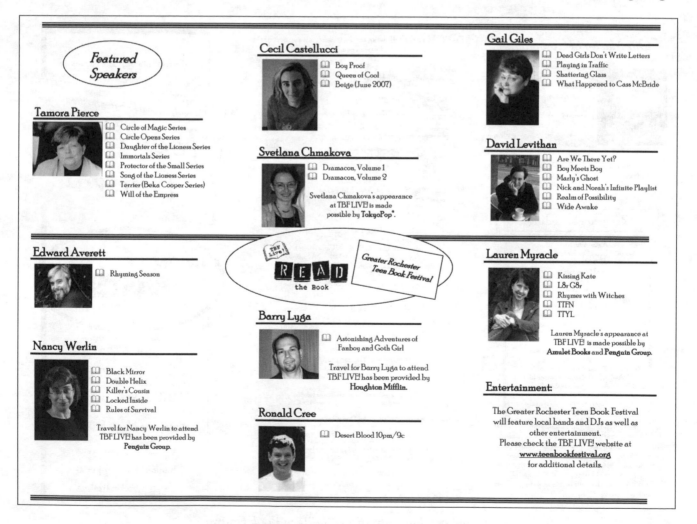

Featured Speakers

Tamora Pierce
- Circle of Magic Series
- Circle Opens Series
- Daughter of the Lioness Series
- Immortals Series
- Protector of the Small Series
- Song of the Lioness Series
- Terrier (Beka Cooper Series)
- Will of the Empress

Cecil Castellucci
- Boy Proof
- Queen of Cool
- Beige (June 2007)

Svetlana Chmakova
- Dramacon, Volume 1
- Dramacon, Volume 2

Svetlana Chmakova's appearance at TBF LIVE! is made possible by TokyoPop®.

Gail Giles
- Dead Girls Don't Write Letters
- Playing in Traffic
- Shattering Glass
- What Happened to Cass McBride

David Levithan
- Are We There Yet?
- Boy Meets Boy
- Marly's Ghost
- Nick and Norah's Infinite Playlist
- Realm of Possibility
- Wide Awake

Edward Averett
- Rhyming Season

Nancy Werlin
- Black Mirror
- Double Helix
- Killer's Cousin
- Locked Inside
- Rules of Survival

Travel for Nancy Werlin to attend TBF LIVE! has been provided by Penguin Group.

TBF Live! READ the Book — Greater Rochester Teen Book Festival

Barry Lyga
- Astonishing Adventures of Fanboy and Goth Girl

Travel for Barry Lyga to attend TBF LIVE! has been provided by Houghton Mifflin.

Ronald Cree
- Desert Blood 10pm/9c

Lauren Myracle
- Kissing Kate
- L8r G8r
- Rhymes with Witches
- TTFN
- TTYL

Lauren Myracle's appearance at TBF LIVE! is made possible by Amulet Books and Penguin Group.

Entertainment:

The Greater Rochester Teen Book Festival will feature local bands and DJs as well as other entertainment. Please check the TBF LIVE! website at www.teenbookfestival.org for additional details.

valuable feedback. Evaluations collected at the 2006 TBF helped select authors to invite and make improvements in 2007. In addition to participating in numerous fundraisers, teens helped make chocolate beforehand to put in hospitality bags for the authors and decorated library book pocket cards for them with messages of welcome and gratitude.

On the day of the festival, young adults arrived to set up the building two hours ahead of time. They ran errands, put up posters, hauled boxes, and performed other physically intensive tasks. When the authors arrived in a limousine, the teens were gathered outside the high school on both sides of a red carpet and stanchions, screaming and clapping as their favorite writers entered the building. Besides attending the event, some teen volunteers are given the task of escorting the authors, introducing them at their breakout sessions, and providing assistance to the authors during autographing sessions. For these students, one of the highlights for them is eating breakfast with that author before the festival begins. Some teens were given the job of "paparazzi," which involved roaming throughout the building with cameras and taking pictures.

The plannin committee wanted the entertainment to be "by teens, for teens." In 2006, a high school step team from the Rochester City School District performed. In 2007, the local teen band Aistera played to kick off the festival. Both years, the DJ club from Minerva DeLand School in Fairport provided music throughout the day in the gymnasium.

Many young adults stayed to clean up the building at the end of the day, well after the authors had departed. Without these numerous and enthusiastic volunteers, the TBF could not be accomplished.

Evaluation

Evaluation forms were available during the event for all attendees to complete. As an extra incentive, gift bags with free books from Tokyopop

Flyer advertising Teen Book Festival

were given away for filling out a form. In 2006, 285 sheets were returned, and in 2007, 381 came back. Comments from all age groups were overwhelmingly positive.

Each year the committee tries to improve TBF. The choice of the planning committee members is important to ensure that all are able and willing to commit to the amount of time and work that is involved. All are given clear deadlines for each subcommittee. While having teens on the planning committee was not an option due to the sensitive nature of honoraria negotiations and other financial details, having the teens take more prominent and active roles throughout the planning process in other ways is also an area that is in development for future festivals.

There are many potential variations where smaller schools or libraries could still fulfill the core mission statement of this TBF. Planning could focus on local authors who might be willing to waive or lower their speaking fees. Smaller events could have fewer authors or a different schedule that would not involve simultaneous breakout sessions, or utilize a less structured day involving a few planned presentations by select authors, with the main focus of the day being casual interaction with authors. For events strictly within a school setting, the mission could be changed to make it more curriculum-based, perhaps with one author visiting each school in a district on the same day. For larger events, more authors or entertainment could be solicited to make it a multi-day event. Another variation could include charging to attend the event to help offset costs. Some fee structures could be created, with teens paying less than adults.

A selection of comments from TBF participants:

> The speeches really moved me. I may consider a career as an author. (age 12)

> I like being exposed to the new types of books. I also really enjoyed meeting and talking to the authors, they all seemed really nice and I liked asking them questions. (age 17)

> The author sessions were amazing and hanging out with my friends. It was a great chance to express my fandom. (age 15)

A selection of author testimonials:

> If you're an author and you want an excuse to have a good time while also meeting some of the best librarians and fans in the world, I have one piece of advice: Hie thee to the Teen Book Festival! There's nothing quite like the excitement and enthusiasm of the readers in Rochester. TBF means lots of fans, great publicity, and rock star treatment that authors probably don't deserve . . . but will happily lap up!"—Barry Lyga

If the idea of a teen book festival doesn't strike you as uproariously fun, you haven't been to the Rochester Teen Book Festival. This is the Woodstock of YA lit!—Ellen Wittlinger

I've given a lot of thought to the festival. What I loved most about it was the atmosphere of friendship that flowed through it. There was no "us" vs. "them." No outsiders. We were all insiders, all of us who are passionate about good books; the kids, librarians, parents, teachers, authors. We all connected through the love of story. For a few hours, we filled the safest place in the world. I wish I could have captured the feeling and bottled it.

> You set the gold standard for author treatment. We all have horror stories. . . . I'll spare you the details, but they are ugly. I really felt that my work was being honored and my spirit respected. I am sure all of the other speakers would echo that. My energy level stayed high through the day. (Doesn't always happen!) I really enjoyed the opportunities you provided for all of the speakers to hang out together. That was very nice.—Laurie Halse Anderson

Relevance to Overall Young Adult Services

The mission statement on the TBF Web site reads: "The mission is to foster a community effort to celebrate and promote reading by connecting teens and authors." The Greater Rochester Teen Book Festival helps move beyond library and school walls to get in touch with young adults. Some of the attendees came only to see the performers, but ultimately found an author that sparked their interest. Seeing these teens excited about reading as they mingled with other young people from different areas made all of the planning worthwhile, and truly achieved the goals.

Anti-Prom

**Nathan Straus Teen Central, Donnell Library Center,
New York Public Library, New York, New York**

Type of program/service:
Single program/special event

Targeted audiences:
Middle School, Junior High, Senior High

Name of contact person:
Megan Honig, mhonig@nypl.org

Program Summary

Anti-Prom is a dance party, author event, and celebration of young adult participation in the library rolled into one evening. Organized with the help of a motivated Teen Advisory Group, the event is held on a weekday evening near the end of the school year. Teen Central is decorated according to the Anti-Prom theme, which is selected by the Teen Advisory Group. Themes have included Blue Hawaii (2005), Memoirs of Teen Central (as in *Memoirs of a Geisha*, 2006) and Heaven and Hell (2007). Young adults are invited to mingle, dance, and eat snacks and a light dinner. A guest author (Christopher Krovatin, 2006; James St. James, 2007) speaks. Participants choose a king and queen. Volunteers take digital photographs. Attendees receive goody bags full of buttons, bookmarks, and galleys donated by publishers as well as flyers and brochures promoting library events.

Steps

The two most important aspects of preparation for the Anti-Prom are youth participation and volunteer recruitment. Teen Advisory Groups or other teen library users can and should make decisions about the event: What is the theme? What music should be played? What should the invitations look like? Young adults who are invested in the program can also publicize the event.

Volunteers are also essential. Volunteers chaperone, serve dinner, mix punch, take photographs, and monitor the event. Publishers and local businesses can donate goody bag prizes and a guest author can serve as a focal point for the evening (as well as a tie-in to library collections!).

Decorations, snacks, beverages, cups, and plenty of napkins should be purchased. Dinner can be ordered for delivery. Make sure to arrange furniture so that there is a table for food service and a space for dancing!

Description of Library

Billed as "a space of your own in Midtown Manhattan," Teen Central is the flagship social, educational, and recreational space for young adult services in the New York Public Library. Separated from quieter areas of the Donnell Library Center by soundproof glass and wall-to-wall carpeting, Teen Central is outfitted with a speaker system, a big-screen TV, and twelve Internet computers. Computers, tables, and lounge chairs are all reserved for patrons between ages 12 and 18. A quiet study room is available for patrons who prefer to work quietly. Teen Central features a large collection of popular CDs, DVDs, magazines, graphic novels, and approximately 25,000 fiction and nonfiction books for leisure reading, homework help, and college and career guidance. An active Teen Advisory Group provides weekly input and feedback on programs and materials.

Intended Audience and Demographics

Teen Central is a destination for young adults throughout New York City. The city teens are an extremely diverse group. Of the 8.1 million New York City residents, approximately 2 million are under 18. Of these 2 million, about 850,000 are between the ages of 10 and 18. New York City teens hail from a variety of racial and socioeconomic backgrounds, including many immigrant families and those living in poverty. Additionally, Teen Central currently sees many anime and manga fans; self-identified goths or those with a goth aesthetic; and gay, lesbian, bisexual, transgender, and questioning (GLBTQ) teens. Anti-Prom, like Teen Central itself, is open to all young adults in New York City, ages 12 to 18.

Rationale

In contemporary American high schools, the prom is an almost mythological rite of passage. Some young adults are not able to enjoy or participate in their own school's prom for reasons including age, finances, or intolerance. Anti-Prom celebrates all young adults, including GLBTQ teens, those interested in anime and goth fashion, and those in financial need. Unlike traditional proms, Anti-Prom is a free event, and attendance is not limited to juniors and seniors. Formal dress is not required, although attendees are invited to dress up according to their own sense of style. In contrast to traditional promgoers, Anti-Prom attendees are encouraged to arrive alone or with friends. In 2006 the Anti-Prom's king and queen were both out GLBTQ teens who had made significant contributions to Teen Central over the preceding year.

Like Teen Central itself, Anti-Prom provides opportunities for young adults from all parts of New York City to interact with each other outside of their usual social groups as well as with young adult librarians and authors. Anti-Prom also promotes library use and leisure reading by: inviting guest authors; providing goody bags full of bookmarks, buttons, galleys, and flyers advertising future library events; and showing the library to be a fun, creative, and responsive space for young adults.

Number of Young Adults Reached

One hundred young adults attended the first Anti-Prom in 2005, and seventy-five attended in 2006. Attendance is expected to grow because of an increased number of young adult librarians promoting Anti-Prom to Teen Advisory Groups and to individual young adults in neighborhood branches.

Number of Staff and Volunteers

The four librarians and one administrative assistant on staff at Teen Central plan and implement Anti-Prom. Young adult librarians from neighborhood branches of the New York Public Library are invited to volunteer as chaperones and to encourage young adults from their own neighborhoods to attend.

Funding and Budget Figures

Anti-Prom has a budget of approximately $350 for dinner, snacks, and decorations. Four full-time members and one part-time staff member of Teen Central each spend approximately four hours planning and four hours implementing the event (at approximately $25 each per staff hour). Funding for food and decorations came from a grant from the Wallace Foundation in 2005, the Cultural After School Adventure Program by New York City Council Member Christine Quinn and the City of New York in 2006, and internal New York Public Library funds for young adult services in 2007. Guest authors and chaperones volunteer their time, and publishing houses including Penguin Putnam, MTV Books, Simon & Schuster, First Second Books, and Tokyopop donate promotional materials for goody bags.

Marketing

Invitations and word of mouth are the primary means for promoting Anti-Prom. Invitations for 2007's Anti-Prom featured an eye-catching manga-style drawing and a cover image of *Freak Show* by guest author James St. James. Invitations are sent to libraries throughout the New York Public Library system for distribution to young adults in neighborhood libraries and local schools. A copy of the invitation also appeared on the home page of Teenlink, the New York Public Library's Web site for young adults, and a link to the invitation appeared in the "news" section of the NYPL home page. Regular visitors of Teen Central also promote the event to friends by word of mouth.

Youth Participation

Youth participation is central to planning Anti-Prom. Every year, Teen Central's Teen Advisory Group helps create the Anti-Prom playlist, suggest favorite snacks, and selects the Anti-Prom theme. The invitation for 2007's Heaven and Hell Anti-Prom, featuring a manga-style angel and devil floating above the words "Abandon All Hope," was drawn by a longtime Teen Advisory Group member. The Teen Advisory Group continues to generate creative ideas for Anti-Prom. Newest ideas include healthy snacks, face painting, and selecting Anti-Prom's king and queen without regard to the winners' gender.

Evaluation

The popularity of Anti-Prom year after year is a testament to the event's success. As the event approaches, regular visitors to Teen Central eagerly ask when Anti-Prom will be held and tell librarians that they will attend and invite friends. After the event, young adults are eager to see the pictures that have been taken at Anti-Prom. Even as much as a year or two later teens will continue to view Anti-Prom digital slideshows. Most after-school programs at Teen Central see ten to twenty participants, but seventy-five to one hundred young adults attend Anti-Prom.

Other libraries considering planning this event should enlist teen input on theme, music, and voting for the king and queen. The form may indicate to teens that "I nominate _____ for _____ because _____". A chaperone should check that each person has voted once! It is also important to assign a chaperone to watch the food so some is available all evening long.

Relevance to Overall Young Adult Services

Anti-Prom celebrates the contributions of Teen Central's Teen Advisory Group while reaching out to young adults across New York City. Young adults who may be unfamiliar with Teen Central are given a chance to experience the library resources and unique space. In addition, young adult attendees have the opportunity to interact socially with each other and with adults, including librarians and authors. The timing of Anti-Prom at the end of the school year is also important: Attendees inspired by Anti-Prom often return to Teen Central during the summer months for summer reading club meetings, author programs, and to volunteer their services, or just hang out and enjoy the library on a long, hot day.

Resources

Martin Jr., Hillias J., and James R. Murdock. *Serving Lesbian, Gay, Bisexual, Transgender, and Questioning Teens: A How-To-Do-It Manual for Librarians.* New York: Neal-Schuman, 2007.

Pbwiki.com (for keeping everything organized!)

San José Teen Idol

San José Public Library, San Jose, California

Type of program/service:
Single program/special event

Targeted audiences:
Junior High, Senior High

Name of contact person:
Angie Miraflor, angie.miraflor@sjlibrary.org

Other category:
Living in a Diverse World

Program Summary

San José Public Library (SJPL) held its first San José Teen Idol singing contest, attracting 150 teen contestants and 1,000 audience members to the library. Participants showed off their vocal talent, gained experience performing in public, while learning the value of friendly competition for prizes. All eighteen libraries held local competitions with $50, $25, and $10 prizes. Library staff, teen volunteers, and community members judged the performances on vocal ability and stage presence. Contestants could sing in any language or genre, and the selected songs ranging from folk music to pop hits to show tunes. The winners of each branch competed at a grand finale held at the main library for a grand prize of $500.

Steps

In April 2007, all branch libraries and the main library held regional competitions. They were not held on the same day. Each branch took signups for their program. When a teen signed up for the competition, they also received the rules and a photo release form in case they would then be posted on the Web site.

During the day of the events, teen volunteers helped decorate the stage for the performers, performed crowd control, made sure all of the singers checked in and helped with other needed logistics. Some of the branches used microphones or karaoke machine microphones, while other branches had an intimate enough setting for the singers to sing without any microphones.

The judges were different at each branch. Some of the judges included Teen Advisory Group members, staff members, music teachers, and friends of volunteers. Each branch had at least three judges. Each person sang for two minutes and judges scored them using a scoring sheet the San José Idol committee created. At the end of the program, the top three winners were announced and the cash prizes were given. The winner was then told that they were going to compete at the final competition at the main library to be held in May.

The grand finale competition was held toward the end of May. For this event a stage was set up. The audiovisual department provided speakers and a podium, and it was held in the large library lobby. One of the librarians dressed up in his tuxedo to emcee the event. Programs were also handed out that included a timeline of the event, the list of the contestants, their ages, and a quote from them about why they like to sing or how they started performing.

The judges for the main competition were members of the City of San José Youth Commission.

Promotional materials were made for all of the branches for consistency. The library marketing staff member promoted the branch events, winners, and final event. Local coverage was also promoted through newspapers, Internet news sites, and radio announcements.

The best part about the program was that it was very flexible for each branch. Basic rules were developed for the contest, but each branch could cater it to fit their own community needs. Some branches had large community rooms and high-tech audio equipment while others had to simply block off library space for the program. All turned out very well.

Description of Library

San José Public Library, located on the central California coast, is the largest public library system between San Francisco and Los Angeles, serving a population of 953,000. A proud recipient of the 2004 *Gale/Library Journal* Library of the Year Award, the library is an acknowledged leader in providing innovative services to meet changing customer needs. A multiethnic and culturally diverse community is served by the Dr. Martin Luther King Jr. Main Library and seventeen branches. The King Library is the only library in the country that is co-owned and operated by a major metropolitan university and a major city. In November 2000, voters approved a $212 million branch development bond project. By the end of this project, all branches will be renovated and an additional five branches will be added to the system for a total of twenty-three branches.

Intended Audience and Demographics

The target audience was teens 12- to 19- years-old living in San José, but teens from neighboring cities competed as well, bringing in some customers who had never visited a San José library. According to the 2005 U.S. Census, the population of 12- to 19-year olds in San José is 97,606. This number represents 11 percent of the city's total population. San José's top three ethnic groups are Latino (31 percent), Asian (30 percent), and Caucasian (18 percent). According to Kidsdata.org, in 2005, 65.7 percent of high school graduates completed college preparatory courses and there was a high school drop out rate of 7.3 percent.

Rationale

Although a singing competition may not be the first program to come to mind when it comes to library services, it complements the core goal of San José Public Library: to provide a place for life-long learning. Whether the teens have taken singing lessons for years or just recently discovered their vocal talent, the program provided a safe, fun place for teens to express themselves. This program brought teens who had never stepped into a San José library, and it also involved the teens who were in the library, but never participated in a program. San José Teen Idol also proved to be a way for teens to learn from and participate in healthy competition. Participants learned such skills as public performance and self-marketing that will serve them in their future academic and career goals.

Number of Young Adults Reached

One hundred and fifty teens competed in the branch events. There were eighteen contestants at the final event, with many teens bringing groups of friends and family to cheer them on. The total number of audience members at all of the branch competitions was 900 and the final event had an audience of 260. In addition, the competitions were staffed by members of TeensReach, the San José Public Library corps of teen volunteers. TeensReach volunteers planned, publicized, judged, and evaluated the events.

Number of Staff and Volunteers

At least one librarian planned each of the local competitions, and other library staff helped with the set up and judging during the program. The volunteers had a number of roles including judges, decorators, competition MCs, and advertisers. With the exceptions of the prize amounts and contest rules, the branch competitions were flexible so branches could cater their programs to their community needs and staffing abilities. The planning committee consisted of five librarians who also worked at the final event.

Staff time was categorized as follows:

SJ Teen Idol Committee planning for the branch and final events
(5 members × 5 hours)

Marketing and communications publicity
(8 hours)

Program planning and events at branch libraries: 1 librarian per branch
(18 librarians × 5 hours)

Additional non-librarian staff help at program: 1 staff member per branch
(18 × 1 hour)

Final event program
(4 librarians × 5 hours)

Funding and Budget Figures

The total cost of San José Teen Idol came to $7,360. The breakdown of this total is below:

Expense

SJ Teen Idol Committee planning for the branch and final events
(5 members × 5 hours × $33/hour) $825

Marketing and communications publicity
(8 hours × $30/hour) plus printing of flyers and programs ($200) $440

Program planning and events at branch libraries 1 librarian per branch
(18 librarians × 5 hours × $33/hour) $2,970

Additional non-librarian staff help at program
1 staff member per branch
(18 × $20/hour) $360

Final event program
(4 librarians × 5 hours × $33/hour) $660

Prizes for branches ($85 × 18) $1,530

Prizes for final event $575

TOTAL $7,360

Funding for the prizes came from the individual branches' Friends and TeensReach groups, and funding for the final event came from the King Library's Friends group and young adult programming funds from the King Library.

Marketing

A system-wide flyer was made announcing all of the branch competitions and posted at libraries, schools, and other locations popular with teens. The final event was promoted with a special flyer. Branches posted their competition dates on their Web sites and a separate Web page was made just for the program, linking to the branch posts. Many of the branches also posted their event on MySpace pages. The marketing and communications director put out three press releases announcing the branch competitions, naming the final competitors, and congratulating the winners of the final event. Local media covering the program included KLIV 1590 Silicon Valley News, *San José Mercury News* (the city's major daily newspaper), and the *Los Gatos Weekly Times*.

Youth Participation

From the beginning, San José Teen Idol was a program that came straight from the teens themselves. The idea came from a teen advisory group at one of the branches after they had a casual yet successful open-mic event. When San José Teen Idol was proposed at a meeting of the system's youth services librarians, it was decided to make it a system-wide event. TeensReach, and SJPL's teen Advisory Group provided their branch events with staffing, promotion, decorations, judges, and even the cash prizes. At the final event, members of the San José Youth Commission served as judges.

Evaluation

The evaluation process is ongoing. After the program was over, many teens approached library staff asking whether there will be another competition in the future. Comments and suggestions from the librarians are addressed at systemwide meetings. A more casual approach was taken as far as evaluation from the target audience. Librarians have asked teens if they would like to see this program again next year, and many of the teens have asked staff about it as well. This was the first year for the program, so there are not any statistics for comparison.

The success of the program can be attributed to the staff responding to teen interests. Teens were more interested in the program because they took ownership of it. It brought something that the teens watch, read, and talk about (*American Idol*) and turned it into something in which they could participate. It encouraged teens who never used the library to visit, and it also encouraged teens to visit different branches and the main library. It was an excellent opportunity for teens to work on leadership and team building skills. Many of the teens were judges, participants, decorators, advocates, and planners of the programs.

Many participants also brought their family and friends to the program so it encouraged families to participate in something together, which can be hard when you have a teenager! Some of the contestants were also singing in front of an audience for the first time so it gave them a safe place to show their talents.

For the library, it was a program that was affordable, produced a lot of publicity, and catered to the needs of the smaller branch neighborhoods as well as the larger community.

Some elements of the program may be adjusted in the future. The rule about competing at multiple branch competitions was that if a teen won first place, the teen couldn't compete anywhere else. But if the teen didn't win or came in second or third place, the teen could go to other branches. Some thought this wasn't fair. Staff also felt that more pictures were needed of each event and more publicity given to the final winner after the program.

Staff would also like to seek more sponsors and partnerships. For example, one librarian suggested having the winner sing the national anthem at the local minor league baseball game. The grand prize was large, but the second and third prizes for the grand finale were really small, so staff will adjust that in the future.

Smaller public libraries could run this program by involving their local high schools and inviting winners from each of those schools to compete for the grand finale. Another way to do this would be to involve multiple smaller libraries.

Relevance to Overall Young Adult Services

San José Teen Idol fit into young adult services in a number of ways. One of the purposes of TeensReach is to create programming for the library and this idea came right from a branch TeensReach group. Another purpose of TeensReach is to give teens opportunities to build and develop leadership skills. Teens organized many aspects of the program: promotion, set up, and judging. Lifelong learning is always a goal for young adult services and giving teens the chance to lead the program or participate in the contest allowed the teens to learn about leadership, performance, creativity, and competition in a healthy and safe environment.

San Jose Idol!

Score card

Name: _____ **Song:** _____

Vocal Ability (1-10) _____
Stage Presence (1-10) _____

Total Score: _____

San Jose Idol!

Score card

Name: _____ **Song:** _____

Vocal Ability (1-10) _____
Stage Presence (1-10) _____

Total Score: _____

San Jose Idol!

Score card

Name: _____ **Song:** _____

Vocal Ability (1-10) _____
Stage Presence (1-10) _____

Total Score: _____

San José Idol score card

Application for Fifth Round of Excellence in Library Services to Young Adults

Excellence in Library Service to Young Adults Recognition Project, 2007–2008

Sponsored by the Young Adult Library Services Association and the Margaret Alexander Edwards Trust

---

Application

Purpose

The Excellence Award Task Force of the Young Adult Library Services Association (YALSA) will select up to twenty-five exemplary teen programs/services in all types of libraries to include in a fifth edition of *Excellence in Library Service to Young Adults*. The top five programs will receive cash awards of $1,000 each. Twenty "best of the rest" applications will receive cash awards of $250. This program to recognize excellence in library service to teenagers was begun by ALA Past President Hardy Franklin in 1993.

Categories

The categories of programs/services for young adults ages 12 to 18 that will be considered follow. Please chose the category that most describes the initiative:

1. **Enhancing Teen Spaces, Physical or Virtual.** This includes teen space makeovers, web-based services or programs for teens and/or projects that make libraries in schools and public sectors more teen friendly and/or accessible.
2. **Teen Tech Week.** Educational or recreational programs or services relating to YALSA's inaugural Teen Tech Week, March 4–10, 2007.
3. **Creative Teen Clubs.** Regularly meeting teen groups based on a teen interest or that enhance library or literary experiences for teens.
4. **Promotion of Award Winning Young Adult Literature.** Services or programs that feature any of YALSA's awards: Alex Awards, Margaret Edwards Award, and/or the Michael Printz Award.
5. **Reading Raves.** Unique reading promotion initiatives, in the areas of readers' advisory,

book discussion groups, incorporation of youth participation in library reading programs, services to reluctant readers or special needs readers, etc.

6. **Community Connections**. Programs or services that involve a close partnership with schools, public libraries, or agencies in the community.

7. **Living in a Diverse World**. Services or programs to teens that promote respect for differences and/or reach out to teens of diverse backgrounds, such as ethnicity, language, sexual orientation, learning and communication styles, gender, disability and/or economic status.

8. **Services Under $100.** High impact services or programs that are low in cost.

9. **Special Events**. A program or service that runs no more than twice a year and that has high interest or high impact on area teens.

Criteria

Each application will be judged on the basis of :

- The degree to which the program or service meets the needs of its community, particularly the young adult audience specified. (10 points)

- The originality of the program or service (creative, innovative, unique). (20 points)

- The degree to which the program or service reflects the concepts identified in *New Directions for Library Service to Young Adults* (Jones 2002). (20 points)

- The degree to which the program or service impacts and improves service to young adults. (25 points)

- The quality of the program or service (well planned, well marketed, well organized, well implemented, and well evaluated). (25 points)

Definitions

For the purposes of this application the following definitions apply:

Services—a term for all of the activities offered by libraries for users.

Program—a library-sponsored event, inside or outside the library, which appeals to a group rather than an individual. A program can be informational, recreational, educational, or all three.

Young adults—young people between the ages of 12 and 18; students in middle school, junior high, or high school.

Public library—an agency established by a municipality, county, or region to provide library resources and services to all residents in that jurisdiction.

School library media center—an agency that provides services and programs in either public or private schools. The programs and services can be offered in a single school or throughout the district. They must be specifically planned for students in middle, junior, or senior high schools.

Institutional library—a library maintained by a public or private institution to serve its staff and persons in its care.

Community agency—either government or private agency that promotes the welfare of the audience.

Guidelines

1. All entries must include the cover sheet provided by YALSA.

2. The program/service described must have taken place in 2006 or 2007, or be ongoing.

3. The application must include a letter of support from the director of the public library, the superintendent of schools, or the building-level administrator.

4. Entries must be models of clarity and completeness.

5. Applications must be submitted electronically to ngilbert@ala.org for consideration by YALSA's Excellence Award Taskforce. An electronic copy of the blank application will be available on the YALSA Web page: www.ala.org/yalsa.

6. Supplementary materials (e.g., artwork, photographs, forms, charts, brochures, slogans, logos, evaluations, quotes from participants) may also be submitted electronically. No more than five pieces are allowed. To submit supplementary materials, please do the following:

a. Label each document with your name and document number. For example, Excellence_Gilbert_1of 5;

b. Upload documents (you may upload three at a time) to the ALA site by using the following URL: http://cs.ala.org/upload; or

c. Send each attachment in a separate e-mail to ngilbert@ala.org.

e. You will receive confirmation that your application and attachments have been received.

e. If you have problems or concerns with this process, please do not hesitate to contact Nichole at (800) 545-2433, est. 4387 or ngilbert@ala.org.

7. All applications must be received no later than midnight (Eastern) June 2, 2007.

8. Incomplete applications will not be considered.

Announcement of Awards

1. The libraries selected with exemplary programs/services will be announced by the close of the ALA Annual Conference in Washington, D.C., June 21–27, 2007.

2. All twenty-five of the selected exemplary programs/services will be included in YALSA's *Excellence in Library Services to Young Adults*, 5th edition, edited by Amy Alessio, to be published summer 2008.

3. The top five entries will receive a cash award of $1,000. The next twenty will receive $250 each. Each award will be presented to the applicant's institution for use with teen services or programs.

4. Libraries receiving the cash awards will be recognized via press release, on the YALSA Web site and at a program at the 2008 ALA Annual Conference in Anaheim, California, June 2008.

Program Description

Include the following information with the application cover sheet (see below). Incomplete applications will not be considered.

1. Summarize the program/service (maximum 150 words, double-spaced).

2. Describe the public library, school, or institution that offers the program/service (maximum 150 words, double-spaced).

3. Provide specific information about the program/service. Limit your response to items a. through j. below and to no more than five double-spaced pages, in total.

a. Identify the specific audience.

b. Describe the demographics of the local adolescent population.

c. Explain why the program/service is important, and how the program makes a difference in the lives of young adults and the community.

d. Provide the numbers of young adults reached via the program/service.

e. Provide the number of staff members and volunteers involved.

f. Explain how the project was funded and provide specific budget figures. Explain how these figures were derived (e.g., number of staff hours and cost per staff hour, outside speakers/consultants, materials, etc.). If the project was funded completely or partially by another organization, include that organization's name and address and describe the level of funding.

g. Describe the marketing that was done to promote the service or event.

h. Explain the level of youth participation in planning, implementing and evaluating the program or service.

i. Outline how the program has been evaluated, supplying comparative figures if possible with statistics prior to the program or in the previous year.

j. Describe how the program or service fits into the overall young adult services at the institution.

For questions contact

Nichole Gilbert, YALSA Program Officer, at ngilbert@ala.org or (800) 545-2433, ext. 4387.

EXCELLENCE V APPLICATION COVER SHEET

Applicants must submit responses to the program description statements below.

1. Title of the program/service: _____

2. Name of library system, school district, or institutional library: _____

3. Place an 'X' by the type of institution:

   ____ Single public library   ____ Public library system

   ____ Institutional library   ____ Single school

   School district _____

   ____ Other (Please specify) _____

   For schools, check: ____ Public ____ Non-public

4. Place an 'X' by the type of program/service

   ____ Single program/special event   ____ Series/ongoing program/service

5. Targeted audience (place an 'X' by all that apply)

   ____ Middle School   ____ Junior High   ____ Senior High

   ____ Intergenerational   ____ At Risk   ____ Special Needs

   ____ Other (Please specify) _____ _____

6. Name of contact person: _____
   _____

7. Address: _____
   _____
   _____
   _____

8. Office phone number: _____
   _____

9. Home phone number: _____
   _____

10. E-mail address: _____

11. Category of program/service (please place an 'X' by all that apply but type the word 'PRIMARY' by only one main emphasis):

_____ Enhancing Teen Spaces, Physical or Virtual _____

_____ Teen Tech Week™ _____

_____ Creative Teen Clubs _____

_____ Promotion of Award Winning _____

_____ Young Adult Literature _____

_____ Reading Raves _____

_____ Community Connections _____

_____ Living in a Diverse World _____

_____ Services Under $100 _____

_____ Special Events _____

12. Name and title of person completing the application:

_____

13. Be sure to attach separate letter of support from director, superintendent or building-level administrator.

Nichole Gilbert,
YALSA Program Officer,
ngilbert@ala.org or
(800) 545-2433, ext. 4387

Young Adults Deserve the Best: Competencies for Librarians Serving Youth

The Young Adult Library Services Association (YALSA), a division of the American Library Association (ALA), has developed a set of competencies for librarians serving young adults. Individuals who demonstrate the knowledge and skills required by the competencies will be able to provide quality library service in collaboration with teenagers. Institutions adopting these competencies will necessarily improve overall service capacities and increase public value to their respective communities.

The audiences for the competencies include:

- library educators;
- graduate students;
- young adult specialists;
- school library media specialists;
- generalists in public libraries;
- school administrators;
- library directors;
- state and regional library directors;
- human resources directors;
- non-library youth services providers;
- library grants administrators;
- youth advocacy institutions; and
- youth services funding sources.

AREA I
Leadership and Professionalism

The librarian will be able to:

1. Develop and demonstrate leadership skills in identifying the unique needs of young adults and advocating for service excellence, including equitable funding and staffing levels relative to those provided adults and children.
2. Exhibit planning and evaluating skills in the development of a comprehensive program for and with young adults.
3. Develop and demonstrate a commitment to professionalism.
   a. Adhere to the American Library Association Code of Ethics.
   b. Model and promote a non-judgmental attitude toward young adults.
   c. Preserve confidentiality in interactions with young adults.
4. Plan for personal and professional growth and career development through active participation in professional associations and continuing education.
5. Develop and demonstrate a strong commitment to the right of young adults to have physical and intellectual access to information that is consistent with the American Library Association's Library Bill of Rights.
6. Demonstrate an understanding of and a respect for diverse cultural and ethnic values.

7. Encourage young adults to become lifelong library users by helping them to discover what libraries offer, how to use library resources, and how libraries can assist them in actualization of their overall growth and development.
8. Develop and supervise formal youth participation, such as a teen advisory groups, recruitment of teen volunteers, and opportunities for employment.
9. Affirm and reinforce the role of library school training to expose new professionals to the practices and skills of serving young adults.
10. Model commitment to building assets in youth in order to develop healthy, successful young adults.

AREA II
Knowledge of Client Group

The librarian will be able to:

1. Design and implement programs and build collections appropriate to the needs of young adults.
2. Acquire and apply factual and interpretative information on youth development, developmental assets, and popular culture in planning for materials, services and programs for young adults.
3. Acquire and apply knowledge of adolescent literacy, aliteracy (the choice not to read) and of types of reading problems in the development of collections and programs for young adults.
4. Develop services based on sound models of youth participation and development.
5. Develop programs that create community among young adults, allow for social interaction, and give young adults a sense of belonging and bonding to libraries.

AREA III
Communication

The librarian will be able to:

1. Form appropriate professional relationships with young adults, providing them with the assets, inputs and resiliency factors that they need to develop into caring, competent adults.

2. Demonstrate effective interpersonal relations with young adults, administrators, other professionals who work with young adults, and the community at large by:
   a. Using principles of group dynamics and group process.
   b. Establishing regular channels of communication (both written and oral) with each group.
   c. Developing partnerships with community agencies to best meet the needs of young adults.
3. Be a positive advocate for young adults before library administration and the community, promoting the need to acknowledge and honor the rights of young adults to receive quality and respectful library service at all levels.
4. Effectively promote the role of the library in serving young adults; that the provision of services to this group can help young adults build assets, achieve success, and in turn, create a stronger community.
5. Develop effective methods of internal communication to increase awareness of young adult services.

AREA IV
Administration

A. Planning

The librarian will be able to:

1. Develop a strategic plan for library service with young adults based on their unique needs.
   a. Formulate goals, objectives, and methods of evaluation for young adult ser vice based on determined needs.
   b. Design and conduct a community analysis and needs assessment.
   c. Apply research findings towards the development and improvement of young adult library services.
   d. Design, conduct, and evaluate local action research for service improvement.
   e. Design activities to involve young adults in planning and decision-making.

2. Develop strategies for working with other libraries and learning institutions.
3. Design, implement, and evaluate ongoing public relations and report programs directed toward young adults, administrators, boards, staff, other agencies serving young adults, and the community at large.
4. Identify and cooperate with other youth serving agencies in networking arrangements that will benefit young adult users.
5. Develop, justify, administer, and evaluate a budget for young adult services.
6. Develop physical facilities dedicated to the achievement of young adult service goals.
7. Develop written policies that mandate the rights of young adults to equitable library service.

B. Managing

The librarian will be able to:

1. Contribute to the orientation, training, supervision and evaluation of other staff members in implementing excellent customer service practices.
2. Design, implement and evaluate an ongoing program of professional development for all staff, to encourage and inspire continual excellence in service to young adults.
3. Develop policies and procedures based upon and reflective of the needs and rights of young adults for the efficient operation of all technical functions, including acquisition, processing, circulation, collection maintenance, equipment supervision, and scheduling of young adult programs.
4. Identify and seek external sources of support for young adult services.
5. Monitor and disseminate professional literature pertinent to young adults, especially material impacting youth rights.
6. Demonstrate the capacity to articulate relationships between young adult services and the parent institution's core goals and mission.
7. Exhibit creativity and resourcefulness when identifying or defending resources to improve library service to young adults, be they human resources, material, facility, or fiscal. This may include identifying and advocating for the inclusion of interested paraprofessionals into the direct service mix.
8. Document program experience and learning so as to contribute to institutional and professional memory.
9. Implement mentoring methods to attract, develop, and train staff working with young adults.
10. Promote awareness of young adult services strategic plan, goals, programs and services among other library staff and in the community.
11. Develop and manage services that utilize the skills, talents and resources of young adults in the school or community.

AREA V
Knowledge of Materials

The librarian will be able to:

1. Insure that the parent institution's materials policies and procedures support and integrate principles of excellent young adult service.
2. In collaboration with young adults, formulate collection development, selection, and weeding policies for all young adult materials, as well as other materials of interest to young adults.
3. Employing a broad range of selection sources, develop a collection of materials with young adults that encompasses all appropriate formats, including materials in emerging technologies, languages other than English, and at a variety of reading skill levels.
4. Demonstrate a knowledge and appreciation of literature for and by young adults.
5. Identify current reading, viewing, and listening interests of young adults and incorporate these findings into collection development strategies as well as events and programs.
6. Design and produce materials (such as finding aids and other formats) to expand access to collections.
7. Maintain awareness of ongoing technological advances and develop a facility with electronic resources.
8. Serve as a resource expert and a consultant when teachers are making the transition from textbook-centered instruction to resource-based instruction.

AREA VI
Access to Information

The librarian will be able to:

1. Assess the developmental needs and interests of young adults in the community in order to provide the most appropriate resources and services.
2. Organize collections to maximize easy, equitable, and independent access to information by young adults.
3. Use current standard methods of cataloging and classification, as well as incorporate the newest and most creative means of access to information.
4. Create an environment that attracts and invites young adults to use the collection.
5. Develop special tools that maximize access to information not readily available, (e.g., community resources, special collections, youth-produced literature, and links to useful Web sites).
6. Employ promotional methods and techniques that will increase access and generate collection usage.
7. Through formal and informal instruction, ensure that young adults gain the skills they need to find, evaluate, and use information effectively.
8. Create an environment that guarantees equal access to buildings, resources, programs and services for young adults.
9. Develop and use effective measures to manage Internet and other electronic resources that provide young adults with equal access.
10. Develop and maintain collections that follow the best practices of merchandising.

AREA VII
Services

The librarian will be able to:

1. Together with young adults, design, implement and evaluate programs and services within the framework of the strategic plan and based on the developmental needs of young adults and the public assets libraries represent.
2. Utilize a variety of relevant and appropriate techniques (e.g., booktalking, discussion groups) to encourage young adult use of all types of materials.
3. Provide opportunities for young adults to direct their own personal growth and development.
4. Identify and plan services with young adults in non-traditional settings, such as hospitals, home-school settings, alternative education and foster care programs, and detention facilities.
5. Provide librarian-assisted and independent reference service to assist young adults in finding and using information.
6. Provide a variety of informational and recreational services to meet the diverse needs and interests of young adults.
7. Instruct young adults in basic information gathering and research skills. These should include the skills necessary to use, evaluate, and apply electronic information sources to insure current and future information literacy.
8. Promote activities which increasingly strengthen information literacy skills, and develop lifelong learning habits.
9. Actively involve young adults in planning and implementing services and programs for their age group through advisory boards, task forces, and by less formal means (e.g., surveys, one-on-one discussions, focus groups)
10. Develop partnerships and collaborations with other organizations that serve young adults.
11. Implement customer service practices that encourage and nurture positive relationships between young adults, the library, staff and administration.

Position

As libraries continue to move forward, organizations of all types, sizes, and budgets must realize that warm, inviting, comfortable, and user-centered environments are integral in attracting teenaged users and transforming the role and image of the library. Such environments are essential in encouraging positive use of libraries for recreational activities and education.

Whether building a new library, renovating an existing facility, or working on a minor facilities revamp, the primary key success factor is understanding why teen space is critical. Developing dedicated, attractive, motivating, and teen-oriented space provides a way to create a positive, safe environment for studying, socializing, and leisure activities. It is a way to outwardly and interactively acknowledge teen customers and their needs by supporting adolescent asset development, creating an environment that encourages emotional, social, and intellectual development, and building a sense of teen belonging, community involvement, and library appreciation

Creating appealing teen environments is also an effective way to expand a library's customer base, by appealing to both users and non-users, creating a wider variety of customers from a diverse social groups, backgrounds, and interests. If done correctly, teen space is a very useful marketing tool, enabling libraries to draw teenagers into the physical library space, leading them to other library services such as materials, programming, etc.

All of these efforts provide a path to increasing current and future library supporters. The future of libraries is tomorrow's adults and, believe it or not, these are today's teenagers.

Other key success teen space factors include making teen participation and input a priority as well as a regular practice throughout the planning, design, implementation, maintenance, and marketing of the space and related teen library services. It is also crucial that libraries appropriately size their teen facilities based on community and student population (ages 13 to 18). Libraries must re-evaluate space allocations in their overall facilities and scale them according to demographics, not personal bias. In public library facilities, the ratio of a teen area to the overall library should be equal to the ratio of the teen population of that community to the overall population of that community.

All space and facilities projects should include a well thought-out plan for improvement, including short-term and long-range planning for current and future teen space and services. During this process it is equally important to get buy-in and support from all stakeholders, including teens, staff, faculty, administrators, and the community. And, lastly, think about what teenagers' *need*, not about what adults *want*. In regard to the actual design and décor of teen spaces, a truly teen-friendly space is comfortable, colorful, interactive, flexible in design, and filled with technology. It is important to keep in mind that "teen-friendly" is not synonymous with unruly, unreasonable, impractical, and tacky. Don't make assumptions or let personal biases impact decision making, whether selecting furniture, shelving or display units, flooring, lighting, paint color, signage, and so on. Items should be welcoming, have visual impact, be versatile, and encourage positive, independent use of the library.

Conclusion

Making libraries appealing and important to teenagers is not an impossible task. Library facilities design is one integral step in attracting teen customers and redefining libraries of the future. Looking at teen facilities design in a new light, letting go of antiquated ideas, re-evaluating traditional ways of doing business, and emphasizing customer needs and wants are essential first steps in moving forward in the world of 21st century libraries.

Resources

Bernier, A., ed. (forthcoming). *Making Space for Teens: Recognizing Young Adult Needs in Library Buildings*. Lanham, MD: Scarecrow Press.

Bolan, Kimberly. "Looks Like Teen Spirit." *School Library Journal* 52, no. 1 (Nov. 2006): 44.

Bolan, Kimberly. *Teen Spaces: The Step-by-Step Library Makeover*, Second Edition. Chicago: ALA Editions, 2008.

Harris Interactive for the American Library Association. *Youth and Library Use Study*. www .harrisinteractive.com (accessed Sept. 4, 2007).

Jones, Patrick, Mary K. Chelton, and Joel Shoemaker. *Do It Right: Best Practices for Serving Young Adults in School and Public Libraries*. New York: Neal-Schuman, 2001.

Public Agenda. *Long Overdue: A Fresh Look at Public and Leadership Attitudes About Libraries in the 21st Century*. www.publicagenda.org/ research/research_reports_details.cfm?list=99 (accessed Sept. 4, 2007).

Search Institute. "40 Developmental Assets for Adolescents, 6th to 12th Grades" www.search-institute.org/assets/assetlists.html (accessed June 14, 2007).

The Value of Young Adult Literature

Background

The term "young adult literature" is inherently amorphous, for its constituent terms "young adult" and "literature" are dynamic, changing as culture and society—which provide their context—change. When the term first found common usage in the late 1960s, it referred to realistic fiction that was set in the real (as opposed to imagined), contemporary world and addressed problems, issues, and life circumstances of interest to young readers aged approximately 12 to 18. Such titles were issued by the children's book divisions of American publishers and were marketed to institutions (libraries and schools) that served such populations.

While some of this remains true today, much else has changed. In recent years, for example, the size of this population group has changed dramatically. Between 1990 and 2000 the number of persons between 12 and 19 soared to 32 million, a growth rate of 17 percent that significantly outpaced the growth of the rest of the population. The size of this population segment has also increased as the conventional definition of "young adult" has expanded to include those as young as 10 and, since the late 1990s, as old as 25.

"Literature," which traditionally meant fiction, has also expanded to include new forms of literary, or narrative, nonfiction and new forms of poetry, including novels and book-length works of nonfiction in verse. The increasing importance of visual communication has begun to expand this definition to include the pictorial, as well, especially when offered in combination with text as in the case of picture books, comics, and graphic novels and nonfiction.

As a result of these newly expansive terms, the numbers of books being published for this audience have similarly increased, perhaps by as much as 25 percent, based on the number of titles being reviewed by a leading journal. Similarly, industry analyst Albert Greco states that the sale of young adult books increased by 23 percent from 1999 to 2005.

Though once dismissed as a genre consisting of little more than problem novels and romances, young adult literature has, since the mid-1990s, come of age as literature—literature that welcomes artistic innovation, experimentation, and risk-taking.

Evidence of this is the establishment of the Michael L. Printz Award, which YALSA presents annually to the author of the best young adult book of the year, "best" being defined solely in terms of literary merit. Further evidence is the extraordinary number of critically acclaimed adult authors who have begun writing for young adults—authors like Michael Chabon, Isabel Allende, Dale Peck, Julia Alvarez, T. C. Boyle, Joyce Carol Oates, Francine Prose, and a host of others. As a result of these and other innovations, young adult literature has become one of the most dynamic, creatively exciting areas of publishing.

Position

YALSA is acknowledging this growing diversity by expanding the number of book-related awards and lists it presents and publishes. Audiobooks and graphic novels are only two of the new areas that YALSA is targeting. Meanwhile, it continues to promote excellence in the field through such established prizes as the Printz, Alex, and Margaret A. Edwards Awards and such recommended lists as Best Books for Young Adults and Quick Picks for Reluctant Young Adult Readers.

YALSA also acknowledges that whether one defines young adult literature narrowly or broadly, much of its value cannot be quantified but is to be found in how it addresses the needs of its readers. Often described as "developmental," these needs recognize that young adults are beings in evolution,

By Michael Cart

Accepted by the YALSA Board of Directors, January 2008

in search of self and identity—beings who are constantly growing and changing, morphing from the condition of childhood to that of adulthood. That period of passage called "young adulthood" is a unique part of life, distinguished by unique needs that are at minimum physical, intellectual, emotional, and societal in nature.

By addressing these needs, young adult literature is made valuable not only by its artistry but also by its relevance to the lives of its readers. And by addressing not only their needs but also their interests, the literature becomes a powerful inducement for them to read, another compelling reason to value it, especially at a time when adolescent literacy has become a critically important issue. The Alliance for Excellent Education has declared a "literacy crisis among middle and high school students" in the wake of research from the National Assessment of Educational Progress that finds 65 percent of graduating high school seniors and 71 percent of America's eighth graders are reading below grade level.

As literacy has become another developmental need of young adults, organizations like the International Reading Association (IRA) and the National Council of Teachers of English (NCTE) have begun to recognize the imperative need for "a wide variety of reading material that they [young adults] can and want to read," (IRA) books that "should be self-selected and of high interest to the reader" (NCTE)—in short, young adult books.

As a literature of relevance that meets developmental needs—including literacy skills—young adult literature also becomes a developmental *asset*, which YALSA's *New Directions For Library Service To Young Adults* defines as "a factor promoting positive teenage development." The independent, nonprofit Search Institute offers a framework of forty such developmental assets.

YALSA finds another of the chief values of young adult literature in its capacity to offer readers an opportunity to see themselves reflected in its pages. Young adulthood is, intrinsically, a period of tension. On the one hand, young adults have an all-consuming need to belong. But on the other, they are also inherently solipsistic, regarding themselves

as being unique, which for them is not cause for celebration but, rather, for despair. For to be unique is to be unlike one's peers, to be "other," in fact. And to be "other" is to not belong but, instead, to be outcast. Thus, to see oneself in the pages of a young adult book is to receive the reassurance that one is not alone after all, not other, not alien but, instead, a viable part of a larger community of beings who share a common humanity.

Another value of young adult literature is its capacity for fostering understanding, empathy, and compassion by offering vividly realized portraits of the lives—exterior and interior—of individuals who are unlike the reader. In this way young adult literature invites its readership to embrace the humanity it shares with those who—if not for the encounter in reading—might forever remain strangers or worse irredeemably "other."

Still another value of young adult literature is its capacity for telling its readers the truth, however disagreeable that may sometimes be, for in this way it equips readers for dealing with the realities of impending adulthood and for assuming the rights and responsibilities of citizenship.

By giving readers such a frame of reference, it also helps them to find role models, to make sense of the world they inhabit, to develop a personal philosophy of being, to determine what is right, and equally, what is wrong, to cultivate a personal sensibility. To, in other words, become civilized.

Conclusion

For all of these reasons the Young Adult Library Services Association values young adult literature, believes it is an indispensable part of public and school library collections, and regards it as essential to healthy youth development and the corollary development of healthy communities in which both youth and libraries can thrive.

References

Alliance for Excellent Education. Press Center, http://all4ed.org/press_room (accessed Sept. 28, 2007).

Cart, Michael. "Teens and the Future of Reading." *American Libraries.* October 2007.

Cart, Michael. "Young Adult Literature: The State of a Restless Art" in *Passions and Pleasures* by Michael Cart. Lanham, Md.: Scarecrow Press, 2007.

International Reading Association. "Adolescent Literacy" www.reading.org/resources/issues/positions_adolescent.html (accessed Sept. 28, 2007).

Magazine Publishers of America. Teen Market Profile. www.magazine.org/content/files/teenprofile04.pdf (accessed Sept. 28, 2007).

NCTE. "A Call To Action." www.ncte.org (accessed Sept. 28, 2007).

Patrick Jones for the Young Adult Library Services Association. *New Directions for Library Service to Young Adults.* Chicago: ALA Editions, 2002.

Search Institute. www.search-institute.org.

About Margaret A. Edwards

argaret Alexander Edwards (1902–1988) helped pioneer modern young adult library services. Often referred to as the "patron saint of young adult services," she was one of the first librarians to recognize the specialized services that address the particular needs of young adults.

Edwards began her career as a teacher, earning a BS from Trinity University in Waxahachie, Texas, and an MA from Columbia University. For a few years, Edwards taught Latin in Towson, Maryland, but lost her job in a dispute with her supervisor. She then enrolled in the library training program at Enoch Pratt Free Library in Baltimore, Maryland, where she found her life's work in providing young adults with library services that were tailored to their needs.

Among her many accomplishments, Edwards established youth services in each branch of the library, with YA staff in place at each. She also reached out directly to teens, a tactic that was considered revolutionary at the time: booktalking at high schools, encouraging school book fairs, creating booklists for teens, offering teen-specific programming at her own library, publishing teens' book reviews in a pamphlet called *You're the Critic*, even taking a horse-drawn wagon filled with books for teens into Baltimore's segregated neighborhoods.

In 1969, Edwards published *The Fair Garden and the Swarm of Beasts: The Library and the Young Adult,* in which she reflects on her career, discussing young adult services philosophy and practice with great humor and style. Reprinted four times since, Edwards' book has inspired generations of young adult librarians.

Edwards' work lives on in many ways. YALSA named two of its awards in her honor. The Margaret A. Edwards Award recognizes an author for lifetime contribution to writing for teens, and the Alex Awards (Edwards' friends called her "Alex") recognizes ten books written for adults with specific teen appeal. In addition, the Margaret A. Edwards Trust has helped support many of YALSA's endeavors, including each edition of *Excellence in Library Services to Young Adults.*

Resources and Publications from YALSA

For the most up-to-date information on YALSA books, periodicals, and online resources, please visit the YALSA Web site at www.ala.org/yalsa and click on "Publications" or "Electronic Resources."

YALSA Books

Edwards, Margaret A. *The Fair Garden and the Swarm of Beasts*, Centennial Edition. Chicago: ALA Editions, 2002.

Frolund, Tina, ed., for the Young Adult Library Services Association. *The Official YALSA Awards Guidebook*. New York: Neal-Schuman, 2008.

Honnold, RoseMary for the Young Adult Library Services Association *Get Connected: Tech Programs for Teens*. New York: Neal-Schuman, 2007).

Jones, Patrick for the Young Adult Library Services Association. *New Directions for Library Service to Young Adults*. Chicago: ALA Editions, 2002.

Kan, Kat for the Young Adult Library Services Association. *Sizzling Summer Reading Programs for Young Adults*. Chicago: ALA Editions, 2005.

Koelling, Holly, ed., for the Young Adult Library Services Association. *Best Books for Young Adults*, Third Edition. Chicago: ALA Editions, 2007.

Lesesne, Teri S. and Rosemary Chance for the Young Adult Library Services Association. *Hit List for Young Adults 2: Frequently Challenged Books*. Chicago: ALA Editions, 2002.

McGrath, Renee Vaillancourt for the Young Adult Library Services Association. *Excellence in Library Services to Young Adults*, Fourth Edition. Chicago: YALSA, 2004.

Vaillancourt, Renee Vaillancourt for the Public Library Association and the Young Adult Library Services Association. *Bare Bones Young Adult Services: Tips for Public Library Generalists*, Second Edition. Chicago: ALA Editions, 2000.

Young Adult Library Services Association, *More Outstanding Books for the College Bound*. Chicago: ALA Editions, 2005.

YALSA Periodicals

Young Adult Library Services is the official journal of the Young Adult Library Services Association. The journal primarily serves as a vehicle for continuing education for librarians serving young adults, ages 12 through 18. It includes articles of current interest to the profession, acts as a showcase for best practices, provides news from related fields, spotlights significant events of the organization, and offers in-depth reviews of professional literature. The journal also serves as the official record of the organization. Subscriptions are a membership perquisite and available to purchase for nonmembers. To learn more, visit www.ala.org/yalsa and click on "Publications" on the left.

YAttitudes is YALSA's quarterly e-mail newsletter, which is offered exclusively to YALSA members.

YALSA Web Resources

YALSA on the Web: www.ala.org/yalsa

YALSA Booklists and Awards: www.ala.org/yalsa/booklists

Teen Read Week: www.ala.org/teenread

Teen Tech Week: www.ala.org/teentechweek

YALSA Blog: http://yalsa.ala.org/blog

YALSA Wiki: http://wikis.ala.org/yalsa

YALSA on MySpace: www.myspace.com/yalsa

YALSA on Flickr: http://flickr.com/photos/yalsa

YALSA on Twitter: www.twitter.com/yalsa

YALSA-BK Electronic Discussion List: http://lists.ala.org/wws/info/yalsa-bk

YA-YAAC Electronic Discussion List: http://lists.ala.org/wws/info/ya-yaac